Praise for Jason T. Smith
Outside-In Downside-Up Leadership

"Jason T. Smith is a pioneering CEO leading the future of business. He is part of a whole new breed of business leaders who understand collaboration of strengths is the new innovation. What Jason and his team are doing at Back In Motion is the first such example of what this looks like in practice. In his book *Outside-In Downside-Up Leadership*, Jason shares his leadership story and personal journey. It is a compelling, authentic, and insightful read and provides a much needed and timely resource for any business owner or CEO wanting to take their journey into the full potential of the future of business."

Jeremy Scrivens | Work Futurist and Innovation Catalyst | Director, The Emotional Economy at Work

"Smith has nailed it! It's a new day for the way we do business. The creation of the ONEteam™ model revealed in *Outside-In Downside-Up Leadership* brings a cutting edge to leadership and organisational management. Jason has captured this sentiment in an engaging story, which he had to live through first before he could share with us. Be challenged to think in this new and agile way, and not settle for an inferior traditional approach to leading teams and managing processes."

Peter Irvine | Co-Founder, Gloria Jean's Coffees Australia | Author of *Win in Business* and *Building Your Business, Your People, Your Life*

"Jason's ONEteam™ case study puts you into the mind of the leader as he wrestles and debates the need for change. This book reads more like a journal as Jason finds courage to share power with the team and break away from conventional command-and-control structures. He reveals with bold transparency the effort that leaders must make in constantly refining their leadership culture, workplace design, and operational effectiveness for fast growing organisations."

George Savvides | Managing Director, Medibank Private 2002-2016 | Chair, World Vision Australia | Fellow of the Australian Institute of Company Directors

"Jason T. Smith outlines what many of us know to be true. All our people are leaders in one way or another, yet mostly we fail to let them lead. This is a story of crowdsourcing leadership and an example of humility. Jason shows in *Outside-In Downside-Up Leadership* that by giving power away, you not only empower others, but also fortify your own leadership further. If only more of us would work like this within our teams and organisations, we would all be better for it. Heed these lessons – they are going to help you lead better."

Toby Hall | Group CEO, St Vincent's Health Australia

"Jason is a highly respected global leader in physiotherapy, who embodies the spirit of innovation, authenticity and resilience. His personal story of pain and failure, which inspired the creation of an entirely new organisational model, is a striking example to anyone wanting to challenge themselves and their beliefs to achieve at the highest level. *Outside-In Downside-Up Leadership* is a wonderful leadership journey, documented by a successful physiotherapist, heartfelt healthcare advocate, and exceptional business entrepreneur."

Phil Calvert | National President, Australian Physiotherapy Association

"What a wonderful and refreshing read! Jason T. Smith should be congratulated on such an insightful book – and more so for his exceptional vision and outstanding success. *Outside-In Downside-Up Leadership* fills a missing link for entrepreneurs who hit the wall because of the limitations of traditional methods of organisational management. The practical ideas in this book not only have great meaning for me personally, but should resonate deeply with other executives and leaders who may now choose to create a version of ONEteam˜ in their own organisations."

John Sikkema | Chairman, Halftime Australia | Director of Global Partners, Halftime Institute, USA | Author of *Enriched*

"Organisational leadership is tough, especially in our complex, rapidly changing world. Jason is one of those rare people who has taken the journey from pioneering an entrepreneurial start-up to leading a successful business in over 100 locations. Thankfully, he has taken time to reflect on his experience and has distilled his wisdom into this practical and inspiring book. It will be a tool that leaders and managers in all kinds of organisations will benefit greatly from for years to come. I highly recommend it."

Mark Conner | Leadership Speaker, Trainer, and Author

"Reading this book takes you on a fascinating journey of dismantling and reconstructing your preconceived views on organisational management. Through the lens of Jason T. Smith's bold leadership of Back In Motion, you will be exposed to a radical and innovative shift in corporate thinking. Be prepared to abandon your conservative mindset about organisations in favour of a new, and ultimately more productive model, promoting collaboration and peer leadership."

Professor Lorelle Frazer, PhD | Dean and Head of School, USC Business School | Co-Author of *Franchising Australia* and *Franchising New Zealand* surveys since 1998

"Over these last five decades of observing leadership at various levels, I have concluded that courageous analysis and daring initiatives of change are vital if that organisation is to grow.

Knowing Jason since the first days of Back In Motion, and watching the phenomenon that has become today's great success story, I have seen his visionary boldness, depth of wisdom, and the personal humility that allows him to admit to the need for change. I can, without hesitation, urge you to read and embrace the wisdom of the pages that follow. *Outside-In Downside-Up Leadership* is an extension of Jason's heart. Knowing that, I can guarantee you, you will be empowered to embrace far greater horizons."

David McCracken | International Speaker and Author

"Empowering, entertaining and educational – Jason's latest book *Outside-In Downside-Up Leadership* will start a new vogue of doing business around the world. It's a MUST READ for all business owners, leaders, and entrepreneurs that are serious about taking their culture and organisation to the next level."

Darren J. Stephens | Founder, Global Publishing | Director, The Trading Room | International Bestselling Author of *Millionaires & Billionaires Secrets Revealed*

"Jason T. Smith has provided a transparent view into his organisation and has enabled the reader to travel with him along his revolutionary management journey. His radical, courageous, and visionary new approach to management provides a fascinating insight into what is possible when traditional constraints are removed. A challenging and inspiring read for all leaders."

Neil Angus MP | State Member of the Parliament of Victoria | Shadow Assistant Minister for Treasury | Chair Accountability and Oversight Committee | Secretary to the Parliamentary Liberal National Coalition

"Jason belongs to a rare set of individuals who have been bestowed with unique abilities covering both ends of the spectrum; a clear and structured mind with a high level of attention to detail coupled with creative innovation. Observing Jason's leadership development since his early twenties reveals a commitment to his inquisitive learning disposition and a willingness to make radical, structural changes moving away from traditional mindsets. A passion to help individuals maximise their potential in the workplace, a strong focus on good character, and well-balanced risk taking enables Jason to lead people into new and unchartered waters producing enviable results."

Dan Daniels | Founder and Managing Director, Daniels Health International | Chair, Alpha Australia

"Transformation takes on a new meaning! ONEteam˜ is more than a model or concept. It is a conscious and purposeful choice. Jason's authenticity and humility as a leader shines a renewable light on people development, corporate governance, and commercial growth. He personifies courage – infusing focus and composure. Jason the man, and this book, inspires others to dream, learn, do, and become more. His journey smashes through frontiers where most ask 'why'? A remarkable lived reality of what is possible. If it doesn't capture your heart and mind, re-read it!"

Lloyd Lazaro | International Executive Search & Advisory, Ampersand International

"Jason T. Smith is a phenomenon – a visionary leader with an absolute focus on the execution of a plan. I recommend every learner, every leader, to follow and read everything he authors as he stretches your thinking!"

John Dwight | Non-Executive Director and Business Advisor

50 INSIGHTS FROM A TRUE STORY OF
REMARKABLE ORGANISATIONAL CHANGE

OUTSIDE-IN
DOWNSIDE-UP
LEADERSHIP

JASON T. SMITH

Entrepreneur of the Year

ARK
house

Ark House Press
arkhousepress.com

© Jason T. Smith 2024 | First Edition 2018
jasontsmith.com.au

Ordering Information

Quantity sales – Special discounts available on quantity purchases by corporations, associations, and others. For details, contact the author at info@jasontsmith.com.au.

Individual sales – Ark House Press publications are available online and at select bookstores. They can also be ordered directly from the author's website at jasontsmith.com.au.

Orders for university textbook/course adoption use – For orders of this nature, please contact the author at info@jasontsmith.com.au.

Cataloguing in Publication Data:
Title: Outside-In Downside-Up Leadership
ISBN: 978-0-9756331-7-5 (pbk)
Subjects: [BUS071000] BUSINESS & ECONOMICS / Leadership; [BUS025000] BUSINESS & ECONOMICS / Entrepreneurship; [REL108030] RELIGION / Christian Living / Leadership & Mentoring;
Original internal design by Production Works
Cover design by Simone Geary

This book is dedicated to my beautiful wife, Paulina.

*For more than twenty years, she has journeyed with me
through the great adventure of friendship, marriage,
parenting, business start-ups, philanthropic initiatives,
and community development projects. She has taught me
much about personal integrity and decisive leadership.*

*Thank you for sharing your life with me;
and bringing out the best in mine.*

Acknowledgements

Writing books is fun. Publishing them is not.

There is so much involved in getting a draft manuscript into the reader's hands as a finished book: structuring the content, editing, graphic design, typesetting, proofreading, copyrighting, printing, promotion and, finally, distribution.

For all this, I rely on a team. They must be acknowledged.

Foremost, however, I live to please and honour the Lord Jesus Christ. He is my creator, my hope, my God. I seek to love Him dearly; hear Him clearly; obey Him boldly; and trust Him completely. He is the sun around which I orbit, my primary source of life.

Second only to God, I am indebted to my wife and children. I am fully devoted to Paulina, Lachlan, Sebastian, Morgan, and Shanisha – my family, our tribe. Thank you for refreshing me daily!

Heartfelt gratitude is extended to all of the team at the Back In Motion Health Group who opted-in on the great adventure of ONEteam". You abound in trust, resilience, patience, courage, and creativity. I am convinced that our revolution would have failed with a different team.

I wish to acknowledge Beth Pocklington as one of the early champions of our cause who supported me in the early stages of writing this book. I also wish to specially thank Joshua Moore, Clarissa Whiting, Dan Martin, Jimmy Mackay, Aman Singh, Craig Pritchard, and Manuja Vithanage for recounting to me many of their personal experiences along the ONEteam" journey, all of which helped ensure authenticity in the telling of our story. Some of their personal accounts are shared within the book, albeit their names have been changed to preserve anonymity.

Marie-Anne Rustichelli, Paulina Smith, Beth Pocklington, Toby Hall, Michael Magyar, and Ben Stickland all willingly accepted the unenviable task of becoming my first 'test readers' – trawling through the draft manuscript, giving valuable feedback and gently guiding the finished work. I am hugely grateful for your tireless patience.

And finally, to the whole team at Ark House Press, thank you for your professional expertise in bringing to fruition a text that I hope will serve many in their quest for courageous and innovative leadership.

CONTENTS

Foreword

Jason T. Smith is a remarkable leader. Equally remarkable is the Back In Motion Health Group story from garage start-up to becoming an award-winning, multi-national, franchise brand in allied health services.

Jason's life underscores the truism that any worthwhile achievement requires hard work and overcoming challenge. There is nothing easy about starting businesses. There is nothing simple about managing teams. And there is nothing fun about the personal hardship that accompanies both of these things.

But the win at the end makes it all worth it.

Jason consistently wins because he embraces the pain associated with authentic leadership, entrepreneurial spirit, and uncompromising convictions.

Read his account of the origins of ONEteam˙. Remember, this was only a two-year window in his action-packed career. He is too modest when he describes the turnaround. And he is too self-effacing to acknowledge his own leadership capital that saw this through.

Everybody loves a nail-biting drama, or a plot with a twist. Given this, you won't be disappointed with Jason's story.

But if you are a leader of teams and responsible for organisational culture, don't miss the opportunities to apply these insights and principles in your own life and business. Regardless of whether you employ five people, or lead a cohort of 5,000, the changes revealed within these pages hold the promise of greatness.

Michael Magyar | Non-Executive Director and Leadership Coach | Inaugural Chair of the Back In Motion Health Group

Preface

When I penned my first words of this manuscript, I was 12,000 metres somewhere above the United Arab Emirates en route to Heathrow, London. I recall floating effortlessly among the clouds, slightly nauseated by the lukewarm purée offered as my in-flight meal, and entirely sleep deprived from the time-zone difference. Yet something struck me.

I could only be on a plane, travelling to finalise a new business opportunity in another hemisphere, because my team in Australia were so good at what they did there.

It was a powerful realisation.

I can only do what I love, because the team are doing what they love.

It sounds reasonable, even intuitive. But it wasn't always like this.

For over a decade, I had led my franchised allied healthcare business, the Back In Motion Health Group, with a traditional vertical organisational structure that mostly worked… up to a point, anyway. And then something changed. We set an unreasonable goal that couldn't be achieved through the status quo.

As it's often cautioned, *don't keep doing the same thing and expect a different result.* We needed to adapt our working style. Our organisational model lacked the critical design attributes needed to unleash our innovative potential.

In fact, eventually, it seemed like our team just stopped working.

Our model was unintentionally suffocating talented people through hierarchy and self-limiting position descriptions. Job titles and lines of reporting became discriminatory. Strategy and decisions were mostly formulated in a linear, top-down fashion. Conversations happened behind closed doors. Without noticing it, elitism and class divisions crept into our workplace. People were being artificially designated into executive, management, and support strata. Influence was driven more by seniority and position, than by intelligence and merit. Creativity died.

In short, we lost our edge.

And it was my fault. I was the leader... and it happened on my watch.

While most people smiled at each other as they swiped their access cards each morning, their sense of value and importance was eroding. We were becoming hollow. Our team structure did not enable colleagues to come to work and make their best contribution.

The workplace became dangerous, manifesting in lots of different ways. We suffered diluted vision, fragmented strategy, disenfranchised staff, underwhelming client service, reduced effort, and indifferent results.

It was one of the most confronting experiences of my working life.

Eventually, the mix of certain personalities and egos, left unchecked in our traditional organisational structure, resulted in 'blood on the walls'. Mistakes were made. Lines were crossed. People were wounded. I didn't have to be highly perceptive, or hugely insightful, to notice the demise. It was obvious to everyone.

We had reached a fork in our road. We could clean up the mess, change over some people, and Band-Aid the problem. Alternatively, and less instinctively, we could embark on a vulnerable search of our corporate soul to discover a better way of working together.

For the sake of everyone, we chose the latter.

We didn't just sugar soap the walls or putty up the holes. We tore down partitions. We didn't run and hide. We stood up tall. We took a deep breath, asked ourselves a series of candid questions, and turned and faced each other. It was scary and exhilarating at the same time... and it took the better part of two years.

Our response was not cliché. Sure, we read journals, sought some external advice, and reviewed the case studies of other organisational models. But few ready-made solutions fit our circumstances. And those that did offer valuable lessons, still needed to be adapted and owned by us if we were to assume a new way of life. This was not an exercise in corporate window-dressing or short-term cultural renovation. We sought to re-discover ourselves.

We became *intentional learners.*

We didn't just turn the traditional pyramidal organisation chart upside-down as some have attempted. It wouldn't have worked. We had to turn ourselves *outside-in* and *downside-up.*

This was more about a change in our inner state than it was a governance strategy. Those who stayed became 'very authentic'!

We bounced *forward.* Management literature calls it *adversarial growth.* We evolved through the pain of failure.

Congruent with the spirit of innovation that characterised the change, we gave our new way of life its own name: ONEteam".

We had incited a leadership revolution in our workplace. We found the sweet spot between collaboration and peer accountability. We discovered an authentic and scalable way to give each team member the freedom to do what they love, and excel at it.

And in facilitating this, we gained so much more.

This book is our story… warts and all!

INTRODUCTION

Smart management

Management is a form of technology, and technology is constantly changing. Viewed this way, none of us should resist changes in the way organisations, people, and resources are managed. There is no single way to manage your organisation, except to the extent that you find the smartest technology to facilitate your overall desired result.

Management theories, organisational structures, and corporate models are designed as tools to enhance the experience of real people in actual workplaces. Well-documented and credible examples include traditional hierarchical models, flat organisations, de-centralised structures, inverted pyramids, hypertext organisations, matrix management, and virtual workplaces.

These business concepts and management approaches should be viewed as enablers rather than outcomes in themselves. They should change and adapt to the needs they are designed to serve. They are not best kept static, in case they grow irrelevant to the evolving world around them and the people who work within them.

Traditional, top-down, linear management structures are fast becoming old technology. While some still prefer to use the iPhone 3 and drive a 1977 canary-yellow, two-door Toyota Corolla fuelled by leaded petrol, both are near obsolete.

So it is true for the restrictive hierarchical organisational models. They are slow. They lack connectivity. They pollute the environment. If there was ever a time for them, that time has passed. We know too much about how people want to work in this generation to not upgrade our management technology and enable them to achieve more.

Our organisation, the Back In Motion Health Group, downloaded its new workplace operating system after our old management technology failed us. Software patches and periodic bug fixes weren't enough anymore. A cultural virus had corrupted our code and we were experiencing glitches in everyday processes.

We needed a whole new platform, rather than just a temporary reboot. Our fix relied on hardware and software changes.

The result was worth the effort.

Custom build

In keeping with the technology metaphor, a custom made, bespoke application typically serves you better than whatever you can find on the shelf. In our modern world, we can buy, sort, and compile componentry with relative ease to build the right technology to specifications that match our needs.

The same is true with your organisational model.

While I share the specifics of our ONEteam™ technology in this book, I am not an expert in organisational design. My intention is to promote multiple possibilities that may exist for you to innovate your own workplace model.

We do not consider ONEteam™ to be the right approach for everyone, as much as we believe it is right for us. You too must find what is right for your workplace.

The best hope in finding the right solution for you is to posture yourself as a learner. This is what we did. And the learning curve is still steep, even as I publish this book.

In observing the development of microprocessors for personal computing, Gordon Moore (co-founder of Intel) predicted that the technology would advance twice as fast and cost half the price with each iteration. The number of transistors per square inch on integrated circuit boards doubled every year since their invention until only recently.

In a similar way, organisational management needs to evolve quickly and become more accessible to keep pace with the changing sociocultural landscape. With millennials becoming the more dominant generational influence in the future workplace, they will expect change.

But who is innovating the management process in the same way Silicon Valley revolutionised computing?

We are. And *you* could.

Our journey in building the next-generation management technology for our organisation will hopefully give you valuable insights for your own discovery.

Experiences inform principles

As you make your way through this book, please note the important distinction between *our story* and the *Transferable Principles* that our organisation uses.

I have learned so much in my career from hearing the experiences of others and studying their example. For this reason, I will be very transparent about specific things we did well, and those awkward moments I wished had been someone else's story. Our anecdotes and examples will demonstrate how we have applied workplace principles both successfully and unsuccessfully.

Do not interpret these personal experiences necessarily as empirical recommendations. We share them for your benefit, but not always for your repeating. Learn what you can from our experiences and apply with caution.

Transferable Principles are different. At the end of each chapter I highlight the truisms of organisational leadership – the Transferable Principles – that should not be violated (I have also summarised them in a list at the end of the book). They are like the basic command prompts and lines of software code that every application relies on to succeed. The principles can, and should, be applied in unique and creative ways to incite your own leadership revolution.

In short: learn from our mixed experiences, but follow the principles.

Leadership vs management

The distinction between genuine leadership and learned management can seem blurred and confused when considering historical and contemporary literature. In some cases, it is simply semantics; while at other times, the terms should not be used interchangeably as they mean something quite different.

While it's beyond the scope of this book to deal with all of the nuances of effective leadership, and how it differs from management, the discovery and implementation of ONEteam™ within the Back In Motion Health Group has certainly been characterised by that of *over*-leading and *under*-managing.

The Transferable Principles outlined in the pages that follow speak intentionally to developing personal leadership attributes within colleagues who together make up an organisation, rather than just relying on management structure or protocols to achieve the desired result. Consistent, values-driven leadership, operating within a supportive workplace model, will stimulate individuals and the organisation to flourish. One without the other will result in compromise.

On this basis, please don't be preoccupied with distinguishing the virtues of leadership over the role of management in the early stages of the book. Our story will unpack how I differentiate between the two; and while we believe leadership should always precede management, the two are interdependent and therefore mutually inclusive in achieving overall success.

DIY management

We don't believe ONEteam™ is a finished product. It's not 'set-and-forget'. Our workplace is a living ecosystem that continues to adjust over time as we learn more about how our team works best. It must evolve.

This is both good news and bad news.

The upside for you is that if you don't like one or more attributes of the model we have created, you can consider modifying them to better suit your purposes. You can create your own variation on the theme. Call it 'DIY management'. Find your own expression and courageously experiment. We do.

The downside is that most people are looking for an over-simplified recipe to 'plug-and-play'. We don't offer you a five-step plan to re-invigorate your workplace, or a cute acronym that guarantees a high-performing and self-managed team. From the moment this book reaches publication, it's almost a certainty that we will have leveraged one of the Transferable Principles into a new expression, and pivoted on some dimension of our model.

It's inevitable. As we practise what we have built, we learn. As we learn, we innovate. With innovation, ONEteam™ progressively looks different.

Please remember that while we constantly review our management *technology*, the *Transferable Principles* don't change.

Read with a pen

As we begin our journey together, consider embracing the discipline of *active* reading.

Avoid passively absorbing content. Interact with us. Read with a pen in your hand. Highlight key concepts. Jot down the insights you gain about your own situation. If you think it, *ink it*. If you like it, *write it*.

It's better to rely on a blunt pencil than a sharp mind to remember what matters. Make a list of the actions to follow through. Identify questions you want to ask me or a colleague who is reading the book with you. Challenge the things you disagree with.

Given that it's reported that most people only recall 10% to 12% of what they read, it's a good idea to do something with what you learn. Applying the reading will make all the difference. Build your own library with real experiences.

Remember, a book never changed anything. It's what people *do* with what they read that makes a difference.

Best done in pairs

Find at least one other person to read this book with. Seek out a colleague, supervisor, or employer. Suggest it to an industry peer, or even a business coach or consultant. Engage a mentor. Maybe just invite your best friend.

Put a copy of the book in their hand today and invite them on the journey. I promise that you will get so much more from the experience if you have someone else to bounce the ideas off.

Be warned: some concepts will be confronting, while others will excite you. And you won't agree with everything.

The timeliness of this book is going to be different for each reader. In exploring the Transferable Principles, be careful not to get stuck climbing one tree (let alone falling out of it) and missing the forest.

Minds are like parachutes

Over the years I have encountered an enormous amount of curiosity for ONEteam™, from consultants, potential employees, and suppliers, to competitors, industry peak bodies, and peer CEOs. Their curiosity piques most often when they observe our organisational chart, participate in an internal meeting, hear how we introduce a colleague, or seek clarity regarding who they need to pitch to.

It doesn't take long before they realise something is different about us... *very* different.

Sometimes they ask perplexed questions. Normally their facial expressions say enough.

We have learned that what we do is not always intuitive or simple to explain. For this reason, I have included a glossary of terms unique to ONEteam˜ at the back of this book. It may be helpful to refer to it along the way as you encounter new descriptions.

Some find our leadership model refreshing, and those that don't are at least intrigued. While few people reject the sentiments as being outright unworkable, many are sceptical that ONEteam˜ could exist in their workplace.

We have found it works for us.

Minds are like parachutes: they work best when open. As I share our story, please open yourself to some new possibilities. Make this your story too, and write to tell me what happens next.

1. IDENTITY

Cluedo

It was Colonel Mustard with the candlestick in the library! After numerous interrogations and some nail-biting discoveries, it's a relief to finally declare whodunnit.

We all liked playing the popular murder-mystery board game, Cluedo. It usually demanded time and patience, though, to confirm the right identity of the killer. In my childhood experience, it took approximately 90 minutes on the lounge room floor most weekends.

In the workplace, it typically takes much, *much* longer to confirm the right identity of your organisation.

The corporate world is littered with altruistic vision statements. We marvel at gold-embossed motherhood statements hanging in boardrooms. We pick up full-colour, good quality brochures stacked in reception lounges depicting rich organisational stories. Brand consultants invoice tens of thousands of dollars to help directors and senior management teams discover themselves. Advertisers flaunt succinct taglines full of client-friendly buzz words.

But despite all this, there are familiar, haunting questions that linger. Long after organisational missions have been launched and innovative product campaigns have finished, we ask ourselves questions like:

Who are we really? What do we value that others don't?

What are we called to do? What is our best contribution?

Where can we make the greatest impact?

What is it that only we can do? How are we unique?

These most basic questions help to define our true identity. But, they are deceptively difficult to answer.

One attribute that can never be cloned in an organisation is *inner belief.*

Who you are, and what you value, is crucial. Organisations can copy brand promises, use the same colour palette in their logo design, stir similar emotional responses through aspirational marketing images, and produce a product that looks and behaves the same. But organisations can't fake the DNA within. The values that hang on the walls in the corridors so often aren't lived in the hearts of the workers.

Where the outward may look similar, the complexity and sincerity of the inner world is inherently different in every organisation. We must each deeply understand our own identity. If we cannot do this in a profound and authentic way, then nobody is able to do it for us. For someone to offer any suggestion or alternative would be to project their identity on us. This limits our own personal discovery.

While not immediately apparent to all, every workplace develops an identity. One they choose with intent. Or the one they ended up with by default. No workplace is void of identity. It just may be poorly defined, well hidden, or possibly counter-intuitive. But it's there.

For those who are unsure what their organisational identity is, it's time for a fresh game of Cluedo. It's a matter of discovering what is important to you and why. Define your company's purpose. Articulate a succinct and compelling vision. Agree on definable values to chart your future course.

None of this is a light undertaking. It's a process of trial and error. Don't subdue your curiosity. It's worth the pursuit. You can't afford *not* to do it.

Don the sleuth's hat. Drape the cape. Light up your pipe. It's time to begin the investigation.

Identity crisis

Without clear and articulate corporate identity, teams tend to thrash around in waves of indecision. They stumble through strategic objectives like a sleepwalker in the dark. The culture within the workplace becomes obscure and vanilla.

People who lack clarity, soon after lack motivation. When goals and targets are vague, workers resort to structure, process, and bureaucracy as a form of substitute mission. People do things because they are told to… not because they inherently know why it is important. The *means* is elevated above the *end*.

High performing individuals start to grow weary. Efforts are made in vain. Team meetings become ineffectual. Soon enough, the organisation is without form and void of purpose. Nobody knows why they are there and to what greater good they are supposed to contribute.

While operating under the illusion of progress, the organisation very quickly becomes directionless. Without clear conviction of self-identity, everything stops. At least, eventually. In the interim, teams go around in circles *ad nauseum*. This is the end-stage of organisational identity crisis!

It's no way for any organisation to be. At least, not *our* organisation.

Identity *in motion*

At the time of writing, our organisation has approximately 25 national staff, 70 practice directors, and more than 500 clinical and support staff. We operate physiotherapy practices across more than 100 locations in Australia and New Zealand. We are the largest, and still fastest growing, allied health franchise in the Oceanic region.

Together, we make up the Back In Motion Health Group. Our identity is distinct from all others in our sector. Without this distinctiveness, we would not have flourished.

Of course, it wasn't always the case. Over 15 years our organisation has matured in its self-discovery of who we are and why that's important to the world around us.

It's been a journey. Some would say, a gruelling adventure. Naturally, there have been some triumphant highs and some gutting lows. There has also been confusion and surprise as we oscillated between the two. Every experience has added something to the soul of the organisation we have created. Life has shaped us in the same way the ocean carves its wave-print into the cliff walls that enclose it.

But the journey has not been against our will. We have gone with it. At all times, we sought to preserve and promote our DNA, even when tested under fire.

Intuitively, organisational identity reflects the people within it. It's the individuals who come together and form a collective conscience that imprint on the workplace its culture and *modus operandi* – for good and for bad, intentionally or otherwise. The organisation becomes an interactive installation of those who lead and contribute to it.

In hindsight, I can trace some of the earliest roots of the Back In Motion identity to definable moments during my youth.

Inspirational cartoon

I can remember as a ten-year-old boy eagerly anticipating Saturday mornings.

On the grounds of a carefully pre-negotiated arrangement with Mum and Dad, I would get up early on the weekends and make myself two pieces of vegemite or peanut butter toast. With breakfast in hand, I would then watch the morning cartoons... all by myself.

With the lounge room door closed so as not to disturb my sleeping parents, Channel 9 became my supervising guardian. Slouched in an ugly-brown vinyl beanbag, I became lost in an endless stream of *Road Runner*, *Donald Duck* and *Masters of the Universe*.

By 9am the rest of the family would start surfacing for the day. At this point there was normally sufficient evidence that I had enjoyed a wonderful time, namely a ring of toast crumbs circling the beanbag, and my grin from ear to ear.

There is no way I could know the significance these morning routines would have on my impressionable and formative identity, let alone that of the organisation I would come to lead.

During the early 1980s, as the cartoon re-runs went to advertisement breaks, I can recall seeing appeals for world aid to prevent malnourished children dying in Ethiopia. My field of view went from the crazy antics of an animated mouse setting traps for his nemesis cat, to looking at the stark images of impoverished children about my age. My television set was taken up with images of swollen and distended bellies, lifeless and withdrawn faces, fragile limbs, distressed breathing and collapsed figures.

The children looked unhuman. Many were unable to stand or even hold their heads up to the camera. The adverts captured their plight for the world's attention.

I had no real context for where Africa was. For all I knew, these children were just down the road and around the corner. Maybe they were close, but out of sight.

My little mind flooded with questions.

Why hadn't anyone told me that some people don't have enough to eat?

Who was helping them? Where were their parents?

Why didn't the doctor give them some medicine and make them better?

None of what I saw made any sense to me. It wasn't fair. People needed to do something. With a naive childish response, I decided to help. I distinctly remember sitting upright, staring at the television, and volunteering to support the cause.

It was a profound moment.

I committed my life to helping the children who were dying. It seemed a natural thing to do. In a very unsophisticated and incomplete way, I made a pledge to God. I would invest my life into the stories of others who were less fortunate than me.

It was a deeply personal decision. I didn't tell anyone. I made a promise in secret which took deep root in my heart. And then, Mickey Mouse stole my attention again. Each Saturday morning, during the innocence of my cartoon routine, I found myself recommitting to the cause.

Medical missions

Time passed. I grew and found my rhythm within school. It was not long before I calculated that the best way I could make good on my boyish calling was to become a medical missionary. If I worked hard and was accepted into university, then my practical skills and medical knowledge could be of great service to undeveloped communities around the world.

My heart was set. The mission was firm. Clear identity fuelled my personal motivation and purpose.

Anyone who asked me the cliché question of career aspiration got the same answer. I became known for it among friends, family, and school teachers. I chose my subject electives, worked tirelessly for high grades, and set my leisure-time priorities on anything that would improve my chances of joining the health profession. Whether I was to become a doctor, physiotherapist, or nurse wasn't clear. I was just determined to secure a role *anywhere* in healthcare to work among those who could least afford it.

Eventually, I graduated with honours as a physiotherapist. And I married an intensive-care nurse who, unsurprisingly, shared the same convictions. We were compelled to make a difference in the world together. We had more than enough to share with those in need, it was just a question of how.

We started as volunteers, leading medical teams to Cambodia and India. They were only short-term placements, but each trip contributed to our long-term objectives. We were on our way.

Unhealthy care

During this time, I also completed graduate roles within major public hospitals and worked as an associate in a couple of private practices. These experiences were influential in what came next.

I observed healthcare being delivered in a very reactive, problem-orientated way. There were few long-lasting, solutions-based, holistic interventions. Mainstream medical practitioners were acting more like break-fix technicians, rather than proactive strategists. The profession seemed to be just waiting for people to injure themselves, develop a disease, or experience pain, before offering any help.

This approach violated my intuition. Furthermore, it was contrary to the research literature I was consuming. The world's best practice was informed by weighty evidence. It advocated engaging people in optimal healthy lifestyle choices early, not just offering remedial services *post hoc*.

In short, I became very disillusioned and frustrated, very quickly.

Healthcare was sick. Physiotherapy needed some rehabilitation of its own. The medical professions needed to improve if we were to promote healthy living for our physical best. At least, it was clear *I* must improve.

Convergence

Within the space of a few short but tormented years, my two life aspirations found a common pathway. My pledge to serve those in greatest need, combined with my passion to deliver a proactive model of healthcare, soon gave birth to the Back In Motion Health Group.

These two heartfelt sentiments framed our earliest organisational identity. They seeded our DNA. And even though, at business conception, my wife and I were only a team of two working out of a makeshift consultation room from the garage of our first and unrenovated home, our organisational trajectory was set.

We launched an innovative philosophy of physiotherapy care that redefined health. Our promise was to tailor integrative strategies for those in pain, to help them not only recover from their episode of injury, but more importantly, build a sustainable, optimal lifestyle.

And the profits of our practice were to be given to the poor.

It was a simple idea. But sometimes it's the simple things that work best!

Like-minded people soon joined the cause. Clients were attracted to something different. Staff opted in to the great adventure. Banks took a risk on us. Medical referrals started to flow. New premises were sought. I read a lot of books, asked a lot of questions, and did a lot of navel gazing.

Despite our inexperience in business, health outcomes improved. Results were sustainable. Loyal clients influenced their friends and family. So, the inevitable happened… we grew. In fact, we exploded!

It took a little money and lot of sweat. We stayed focused on our two primary drivers:

1. Empower clients in optimal lifelong health; so that we can

2. Invest into the lives of the poor and needy.

They were exhausting days and sleepless nights. But I had a glimpse of the future. As our momentum built and our results steadied, my heart was quick to dream.

What impact could we have if we achieved a network of 100 practices built on this ethos?

What if every location was led by a values-driven team and aligned to this same core identity?

We would change lives. Probably, whole communities. In time, with persistence and strategy, we might even impact a city, or even the nation.

I buried these thoughts deep in my heart, out of sight, alongside earlier ideas that had been formed many years before during a Saturday morning of cartoons. They remained there unshared for some time to come.

And with that, I turned my attention to the immediate challenges. I had to give thought to organisational design and business models to accommodate our expanding single practice.

MPV₁SV₂

Corporate giants will tell you that *size* is the enemy of *vision*. That is, the bigger you get, the harder it is to maintain congruency. Direction becomes distracted; alignment, almost impossible. Vision leaks and mission drifts. Small organisations are easy to manage. Big ones become unruly, geographically distributed, and less homogenous. So we found out.

We bounced from a single location to six practices relatively quickly. A few years on, and a small cluster of 14 locations existed. In a short time, our organisational identity started to show the early signs of strain and fatigue. Growth brought more people in more places. With volume came diversity.

The heart sentiments that framed my original purpose were not easily translatable to everyone. Some got it, some didn't! It was like the game of broken telephone. To rely on others to convey my passion and values, risked a dangerous dilution effect.

I reacted by writing procedures, policies, and formal documentation. Our organisational structure became increasingly more rigid and defined. Our business was coming of age. It was like entering corporate adolescence. Hormones flowed. Acne appeared. Our voice shook as it deepened. But this was all part of growing up as a business.

In time, we made more deliberate efforts to articulate formal identity statements. With careful wordsmithing and lots of consultation, we captured the essence of our organisational identity in the somewhat awkward acronym MPV_1SV_2.

MPV_1SV_2: Mission, Purpose, Vision, Strategy, Values.

We operationally defined each of these identity attributes in a very personal and specific way for the Back In Motion Health Group. We kept them clear, simple and memorable so they could transfer easily to others. The words took on such significance that they became magnets that drew people together. They galvanised our efforts and minimised our distractions.

Collectively, these **identity statements** became our guiding north star:

- **Our mission** (what we do) is to empower clients in optimal lifelong health.

- **Our purpose** (why we exist) is to be significant to those in need.

- **Our vision** (where we see ourselves in the future) is to be the most loved and trusted provider of allied health services.

- **Our strategy** (how we will achieve our mission) is to provide effective leadership and comprehensive support to become the clinical provider, workplace, and business model of choice.

- **Our values** (the beliefs we are committed to) are excellence, leadership, loyalty, integrity, and significance.

We achieved a certain clarity. The hymn books were passed down the aisles so we could all sing from the same page. We started to enjoy alignment again.

Empowering clients in optimal lifelong health and *being significant to those in need* remained central to our ideology and governed commercial strategy.

We had refreshed who we were and what we cared about. And because of this, growth rolled on.

Self-appointed long service leave

Success often breeds success. But success can just as easily beget failure.

When healthy organisations grow, they require more management, investment, and attention. Back In Motion grew on average between 15% and 40% year-on-year for over a decade. It wasn't long before it was regarded as not only one of the best physiotherapy providers in Australia, but also the largest.

Leading the group became a demanding role.

I was professionally trained as a physiotherapist, not a business graduate. At times, the rigours of managing the business were overwhelming. In founding the group, it was necessary to have performed every role, in every capacity, at some stage. I treated the clients, I mentored staff, I balanced the accounts, I met referrers, and built relationships with local community services. And then after morning tea, I would turn my attention to everything else…

Now I had hundreds of franchisees and staff over more than 40 practice locations, and I was tired. In healthcare, the quality of interpersonal relationships, client service, and clinical results must be of the highest standard. If I wasn't careful, cracks were about to show. It was obvious that I needed help.

I was advised to build a national management team around me. We incorporated marketing, finance, information technology, business systems, human resources, and clinical support. After reading all the books and attending the seminars on popular management culture, I adopted the typical top-down organisational chart to keep everyone in order. It was a traditional linear hierarchy. It was not creative or innovative, just a corporate beige.

Approximately 25 people were stratified into differentiated layers of executives, senior management, and support staff. As CEO, I learned to leverage my time and energy very well through these lines of reporting and organisational responsibility. It allowed me to be in more places at once and hold people accountable for their agreed performance objectives.

While it was a bland organisational model purchased off the shelf, it worked. Our identity did not seem to suffer any compromise. The structure facilitated sizable additional growth.

So, after 10 years, and with things now in order, I agreed to take a long overdue holiday – three months' self-appointed long service leave! Paulina and I travelled throughout South America with three kids under eight years of age. So, it really was just leave, not rest!

7/50/100

Somewhere between the golden sands of Copacabana and the jaw-dropping summits of Machu Picchu, my mind started reflecting. I searched those deep recesses of my heart where the seeds of my personal identity had first taken root. They were still there – nurtured... maturing... but not yet fully developed.

I was taken back to the images I saw as a young boy. Human suffering caused by extreme poverty. I blended with these memories my new graduate aspirations. I wanted to innovate a proactive healthcare model that empowered clients in optimal holistic health.

It was clear to me these ideals still mattered. And I had made inroads with both. Doors were ajar. I just needed to press up against them with more intent.

Back In Motion had kick-started a physiotherapy revolution in Australia. We redefined the contribution our profession was making in the local community. We had launched an innovative philosophy of clinical practice called Results4Life'. We had already delivered millions of health services to grateful clients. We were optimising people's everyday performance and empowering them in healthy living. More Australians were performing at their physical best because of us.

We had also launched the SOS Health Foundation. It is a public benevolent institution focused on improving the health of disadvantaged people living in Australia and neighbouring regions. We were flying health professionals into some of the neediest communities on a pro bono basis, alleviating devastation brought about by poverty and focusing on both the urban poor and remote indigenous homelands.

We were progressively achieving our mission; admittedly, with only little steps. But our identity was still clear. And it seemed our organisational model was working.

But then I challenged myself to think again.

I find I can be more objective when I step outside of my business. Changing your geography can radically change your perspective. While overseas and distant from the daily grind, I risked an old thought for a second time:

What impact could Back In Motion have in the world around us if we established a footprint of 100 practices?

I ruminated on the cute acronym 7/50/100.

This numeric code represented 100 flagship practices, generating $50 million in services, located across 7 states and territories of Australia. It sounded like a commercial target. But it was less about brand recognition, economies of scale, or personal financial gain. Achieving this goal would facilitate human good. And a lot of it!

The business could become the economic engine to achieve our calling in the world. We could reach more people in need. We could offer our signature healthcare model with less barriers. A strong platform of national scale would afford us greater influence to reach out to those who could least afford it.

I wondered, if we achieved 7/50/100:

> *How many more people could we help?*
>
> *Could we manage the growth without compromising quality?*
>
> *What systems and processes would need to be fortified and innovated?*
>
> *Could we sustain it?*

It was big thinking. It would be a doubling of our group in a third of the time.

It dawned on me that we had some limiting factors. Our organisational structure was not fit for purpose. Furthermore, our people were unprepared, and our work habits were incompatible. In short, we were not ready to realise our full potential.

Structure and identity

I was about to learn the hard way that organisational structure must reflect and serve organisational identity.

Ponder this irony. Most organisations have unique identities (albeit in some cases, undeveloped or poorly articulated), but most organisations operate almost identical workplace structures.

This shouldn't compute. Structure imposes itself on every workplace activity: strategic planning, tactical decision making, team meetings, approval processes, and disciplinary policies. Even client service culture is influenced by organisational structure.

If we get *structure* wrong, we risk threatening *who* the organisation is trying to become.

For every unique identity, one must have a unique workplace structure. We should pursue a model of behaviour and workflow that helps us become more of who we really are. Or at least, who we want to become.

This challenges us to embrace the unconventional. Innovative workplaces should adapt their structure to give oxygen to untapped potential – create something new, commission an organisational model that is a press-fit, purpose-designed. Owners, managers, workers, clients, and suppliers will all benefit.

At Back In Motion, we had an opportunity to change – even to be different! Besides, who doesn't prefer the genuine article over a cheap imitation? Our identity was reset around the intention of 7/50/100.

So, it made sense. We were compelled to create a different workplace model to achieve this – something entirely new!

Transferable Principles

1. A clear *identity* will fuel personal *motivation* and *purpose*.

2. Your identity must be *clear*, *memorable*, and *transferable* to those around you.

3. Beware of *vision leaks* and *mission drift*. Organisational *size* becomes the enemy of collective *direction* and *alignment*.

4. A change in *circumstances* often gives you a change in *perspective*.

5. Organisational *structure* must reflect and serve organisational *identity*.

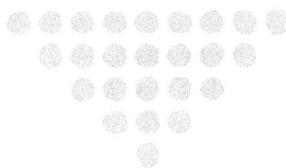

2. IMPLOSION

Limousines and champagne

I bounded through the front door of our National Support Office fresh from my long service leave, on a renewed mission.

While life had continued somewhat humdrum for the team at home, my perspective had changed entirely. I was about to step things up *four* notches. I had my wife's support and the endorsement of the advisory board. It was about to get dangerous.

Elegant invitations were circulated to senior managers. They were requested to attend in black tie on a set date. Curiosity piqued amidst the mystery I created.

When the time came, a nervous gaggle of handsomely dressed staff mingled in the carpark. I ushered them into the luxurious surrounds of a shiny black stretch Hummer. We then headed off through the fog on a cool June morning.

I playfully hosted a pop quiz in the back of the limo. I tested them on the key milestones that punctuated the relatively short history of the Back In Motion Health Group. There was lots of laughter and a few surprises. Before long the sun began to break through the morning cloud. The day opened, full of promise.

Our first stop was an unannounced visit to the first house Paulina and I had bought (and renovated) in Scoresby, Melbourne. This was the location of our makeshift garage practice in September 1999. With nobody home, we snapped a quick photo of everyone standing in place where the first Back In Motion sign had once hung.

Then we were off again. Some time later, we arrived at a secluded chateau retreat. It was nestled among a prestigious winery in the acclaimed grape growing region of western Victoria.

As my special guests entered the manor, there was a large map of Australia pinned at the front of the boardroom. I had delicate gift boxes carefully positioned at each table setting. There were champagne glasses postured for a toasting.

Few knew what awaited. The occasion had been set.

The scoreboard

I noted for everyone present that their successes to date were significant. We had humble beginnings as a single start-up practice. This was similar to many sole trader clinics operating in our small cottage industry. But because of them, things had changed.

We now represented Australia's only franchised physiotherapy network grossing $28 million from 42 practice locations. We had sat in the company of some of the world's most iconic brands on the prestigious *BRW Fast Franchise* list for five consecutive years. We had even been awarded the enviable *Emerging Franchise of the Year* honour by the Franchise Council of Australia.

We offered a superior, evidence-based clinical service. We hosted a world class bespoke technology platform. Our health group was the largest private employer of physiotherapists in Australia. And we didn't look like slowing down any time soon.

From operating initially as a duo with my wife, we now boasted a talented national team. They continued to raise the standard of clinical practice and commercial enterprise within our profession. Driven by an entrepreneurial spirit, we were swimming upstream, fighting Goliath, rolling against the odds, and bucking the trends.

In reflection of these collective achievements, I had also recently been awarded Entrepreneur of the Year for the Southern Region by Ernst & Young.

I quipped with the team that we were an "overnight success… that just took 10 years to create!"

The scoreboard was full! We had lots to be grateful for and plenty to celebrate. And so, we did.

The vision

We raised our glasses and toasted the success to date.

After acknowledging each one personally for their specific contribution, I invited my senior team to be seated in the boardroom of the chateau. I was armed with a carefully prepared slide-deck, a fistful of notes, and a head full of ideas. I ended up just sharing from the heart.

Stating the obvious, I began with an admission that this was not a normal offsite planning session. It was a special day. I initiated with them a conversation that I hoped would build quickly into the next stage of our shared adventure.

I spent four hours introducing 7/50/100. This was my master plan for 100 flagship practices generating $50 million across 7 states and territories of Australia. And it was all to be achieved in three short years. Business commentators call it step change or exponential growth. Most of my friends called it lunacy… even a delusion of grandeur.

It was practically unreasonable. I conceded it would take a miracle to achieve the target. In fact, I was counting on one. It was a God-inspired vision that relied on supernatural intervention.

I tried to explain the newfound passion for further scale. I offered insights from my own personal journey. I meticulously outlined the anticipated geographical footprint of every new practice. I spoke on the virtues of franchising excellence. I shared warnings about the assumptions and limitations we put on ourselves. And I pre-empted some of their personal objections.

My ideas were big. The challenges were complex. The emotion was high. Our time was short. I conceded with the team that I didn't have all the answers yet to solve the riddle of explosive growth. This wasn't to deter us. Necessity would become the mother of invention. As would be their valued and much needed creativity.

This was a defining moment in the identity of our organisation. It became our calling.

Chris's story

One of the absolute highlights of my time at Back In Motion was how Jason unveiled his plans for the strategic season of 7/50/100. I particularly loved the theatre of being picked up in a limousine, the nostalgia of visiting the place where the health group began, and even the nice touch of the black-tie dress code.

To top it off, there was the mystique of where the idea came from and how it was translated into a clear direction for us to follow.

As an employee, I want to feel inspired and motivated by the vision and direction of the organisation. The way that we were brought into the story by Jason definitely made me feel like I could contribute to the strategic plan in a meaningful way.

I also liked that Jason drew a line in the sand. As employees, we were respectfully challenged to either jump on the bus and commit to the three-year plan, or hop off at the next stop. This became a bit of a catchcry throughout the three-year period and resonated deeply with me.

I don't think I've ever bought into an organisational vision and strategy as much as I have with 7/50/100. It was a great example of quality leadership.

The bombshell

And then I stepped onto sacred turf. I boldly announced that if we were to achieve something new and different, then we had to behave in new and different ways. Importantly, the shape and function of our team needed to change.

As I shared with you in Chapter 1, organisational identity must inform and influence organisational structure. An ancient text cautions, *do not put new wine into an old wineskin, lest it should tear and spill.* I was informing our team that the assignment had changed. I was no longer content with organic growth. We were chasing a step-change in trajectory, performance, and results. Time frames for success were being accelerated. The tectonic plates floating beneath our organisational framework were moving.

A fresh management approach seemed obvious to me – but, as I predicted, not to everyone else, least of all my more senior managers.

Flashback

Some weeks earlier I had already learned that our then-current traditional team structure had shortcomings. Within three hours of returning to my desk, on the first day back from long service leave, things were hitting the proverbial fan. I had four staff report to me on rifts that had developed in my absence between our two primary teams. It had become Corporate Services versus Operations.

I got the message loud and clear: my holiday was definitely over.

A confident and capable general manager led each team. One was time-proven within the organisation and could boast a string of quantifiable achievements. The other was ex-military, newly appointed within the 12 months prior, and already demonstrated much needed strategic intelligence. Our organisational structure at the time mirrored popular models (see Figure 2.1 overleaf).

Figure 2.1: The simple organisational chart
of the national team in 2013

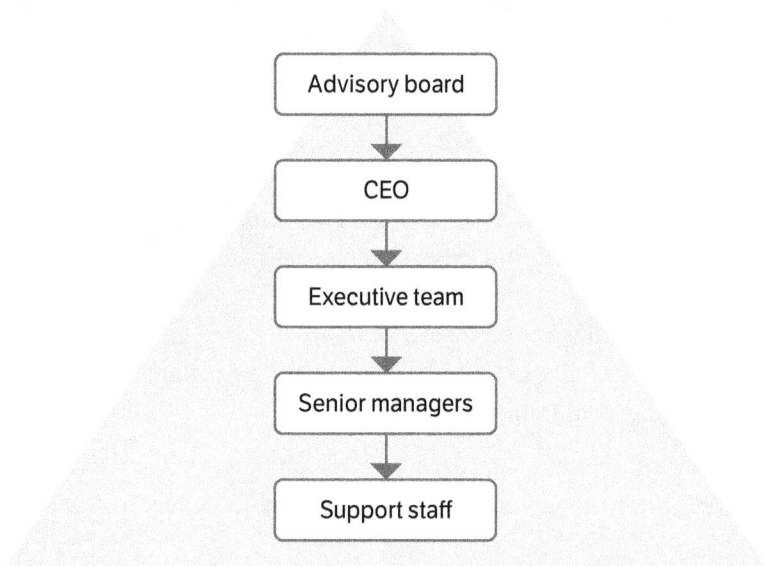

```
┌─────────────────────┐
│   Advisory board    │
└─────────────────────┘
          │
          ▼
┌─────────────────────┐
│        CEO          │
└─────────────────────┘
          │
          ▼
┌─────────────────────┐
│   Executive team    │
└─────────────────────┘
          │
          ▼
┌─────────────────────┐
│   Senior managers   │
└─────────────────────┘
          │
          ▼
┌─────────────────────┐
│    Support staff    │
└─────────────────────┘
```

As the owner and CEO, I reported upwards to a self-appointed board of advisors for external governance, accountability, and strategic input. I then managed the entire organisation through the direct reports of the two general managers: one in charge of Corporate Services, the other in charge of Operations. Together the three of us made up the Executive Team.

Our general manager of Corporate Services was primarily responsible for finance, suppliers, administration, risk, accounting, and technology. The general manager of Operations was primarily responsible for marketing, communications, human resources, field support, franchise development, systems, and training.

Within these two divisions, each general manager had a small number of senior managers responsible for their areas of technical expertise, and support staff who assisted the daily functions.

Together we only numbered about 25 people. Collectively, though, they were responsible for the leadership of more than 40 practice locations and 250 staff in the field (see Figure 2.2).

I always taught my team that the best form of leadership is truth. So we consistently welcomed healthy rigour and transparency in workplace conversations. Respectful candour is essential to identify the best strategies for moving forward. Fierce debate was a feature of most meetings. I liked to encourage opposing views and alternative thoughts in our pursuit of answers.

**Figure 2.2: The detailed organisational chart
of the national team in 2013**

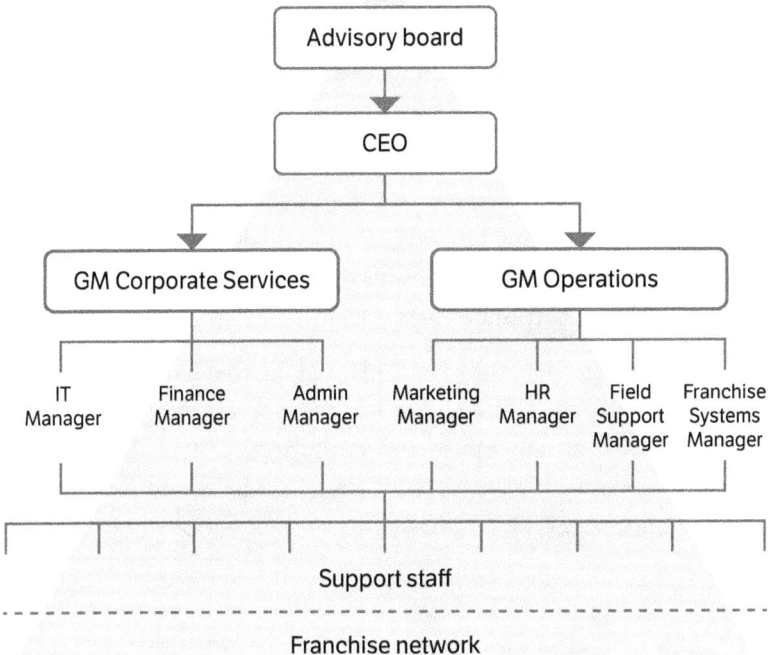

Most people learned quickly how to engage in this style of robust communication and appreciated its benefits. Our people developed the *hearts of lambs* with the *skin of crocodiles* – the right combination, in my opinion.

The problem was, the mood had now turned. The staff were not experiencing constructive confrontation. It seemed the team were at odds. They had apparently lost the respectfulness that afforded the candour. One without the other was poison. Our once positive culture was showing cracks. Tensions were obvious, despite denials from the two top men.

I became quietly concerned.

While the cat's away...

It was clear to me that the executive authorities I had delegated to cover my long service leave had unintentionally given rise to a new form of management style… an unwanted one – *uber*-egocentricity. Otherwise known as *command and control* in formal management parlance.

No one person was to blame – other than possibly myself. Our organisational structure favoured this approach. It was top-down and linear. It stratified people into layers and, by its nature, created a pecking order – a corporate caste system.

The roots of this structure were planted in the industrial age. At such time it was considered acceptable, if not advantageous, to rule employees with an autocratic and authoritative style. It facilitated order out of chaos. It gave workers direction. It created productivity out of inefficiency.

It was a paradigm that worked in its day. But society had matured. It was a *new* day.

For the first 10 years of our organisational journey, we had tried to be inclusive within the traditional hierarchy. But now, some managers were showing uncharacteristic heavy-handed influence. They started to make all the decisions unilaterally, rather than welcoming input. They kept certain reports and information to themselves to fortify their power. They spoke fast, loud, and down their nose. They overruled the suggestions and ideas of others. They greedily accepted all the *credit* and generously distributed all the *blame*. They would speak first, dominate the middle, and always have the last word.

Staff found themselves excluded from projects at the absolute discretion of superiors. Some had their positions redefined against their will. One person even came to work one day to find their computer, files, and personal effects relocated to a smaller desk at the opposite end of the building, without any warning.

Key managers, acting in isolation, were destroying our team – through *unilateral* management. And arguably, because the organisational chart gave them permission to do so.

It got worse. Before long, senior staff would openly confront each other in corridors. They postured with defiance in meetings. They spoke ill of others – initially through the deft art of subtlety and, eventually, in bold outbursts.

Of course, none of it went unnoticed. To out-perform one another and prove their capability, people's one-upmanship began hurting colleagues. It was immature. It revealed a stark lack of inner security and self-identity. It was not the leadership culture we wanted.

Our people were unaccustomed to this style of management. Some were confused. Others felt intimidated. Everyone was concerned. Tensions rose due to the thinly veiled mistrust. Envy grew. Following its natural course, it wasn't long before most felt grievances toward another – perceived or otherwise.

Attitudes are infectious, especially the toxic ones. Support staff felt used and overlooked by their senior managers. The general managers felt unappreciated and betrayed by the support staff. The senior managers became the meat in the middle of the unpalatable workplace sandwich. Some of the middle managers empathised and sided with the younger support team. Others cast their lot with the executive team.

True loyalties were hard to detect. A complex web of psycho-social-cultural intricacies developed.

All this emerged while I travelled abroad. I returned from my leave to a war on the home front.

Spilled paint

But I was back now. Seeing it with my own eyes, it was like watching paint spill. Metaphorically, people came to work each morning carrying open tins of paint. Heavy, black, oil-based, enamel paint.

To avoid spilling their paint, they had to move very carefully throughout the office – give each other wide berths, and walk on egg shells. People were fragile. Words needed to be delicate. Body language was subdued. Nobody wanted to bump any other person for fear of being covered in a messy stain.

Despite their best efforts, nobody could stay clean indefinitely. It was only a matter of time.

Eventually, suppressed frustrations erupted. Words were spoken. Tone and volume became less censored. Facial expressions belied true feelings. Some took licence to say what they thought. Others chose silence over violence. Tensions rose. Relationships broke down.

Paint got spilled in all directions.

Even those who were trying hard to remain neutral got splashed and discoloured. The agnostic could not be spared. The innocent were indistinguishable from the guilty. The perpetrators looked identical to the victims.

We all turned out black – at least, in varying shades.

Incriminating evidence was obscured. The crime scene was contaminated. So I stopped trying to work out who was at fault. I had to own this. *Mea culpa.*

My own hands got marked by the thick paint as I dug around the issues. It became less about who to blame and more about who was bleeding. I instinctively assumed the role of a corporate triage offi-cer. We were barely surviving, let alone thriving.

On the surface, and on a good day, people were still respectful. They could contribute to minimum work flow, and even give the appearance of being 'safe', even though the working environment felt 'dangerous'.

Place any one of them under an ultraviolet light though, and the paint stains were evident.

They were unhappy, felt unappreciated, and were unsure of their future. A little scratch under the surface of the team façade revealed broken trust and growing isolation.

We needed a stain remover. A cultural turpentine to strip the paint. We needed to be cleansed.

Silos

The traditional hierarchical organisational model we had success-fully employed for over a decade was now fractured. It had given rise to different silos, or factions. We weren't functioning as one team anymore, but rather competing against the interests of each another.

In a short space of only a few months, our synergy had been diluted by a factor of five.

We had developed unhealthy opposing identities. Rifts existed between the executive team, senior managers and support staff in the vertical direction. And another fault line opened between the Corporate Services and Operations teams in the horizontal plane.

Five separate parties were now working against each other (see Figure 2.3 overleaf).

It became like the TV show *Survivor*. People formed alliances and protected their backs. Obviously, this changed the way we planned strategy, managed projects, solved problems, and behaved in meet-ings. It even changed where people chose to eat their lunch and who they socialised with. It was a classic dysfunctional team as warned about by Patrick Lencioni in his best-selling book *Silos, Politics and Turf Wars*.

Because our historical team shape and structure had worked for so long, we became immune to its deficiencies and vulnerabilities. We overlooked its flaws and shortcomings. We got complacent. We had mostly good people, but they were now pushing against the very structure that once supported us.

The hierarchical model had a sting in its tale. When left unguarded, it facilitated a very dominating and fearful culture. It permitted some to behave in a way unbecoming of who we wanted to be.

Figure 2.3: The fault lines that emerged in our traditional model

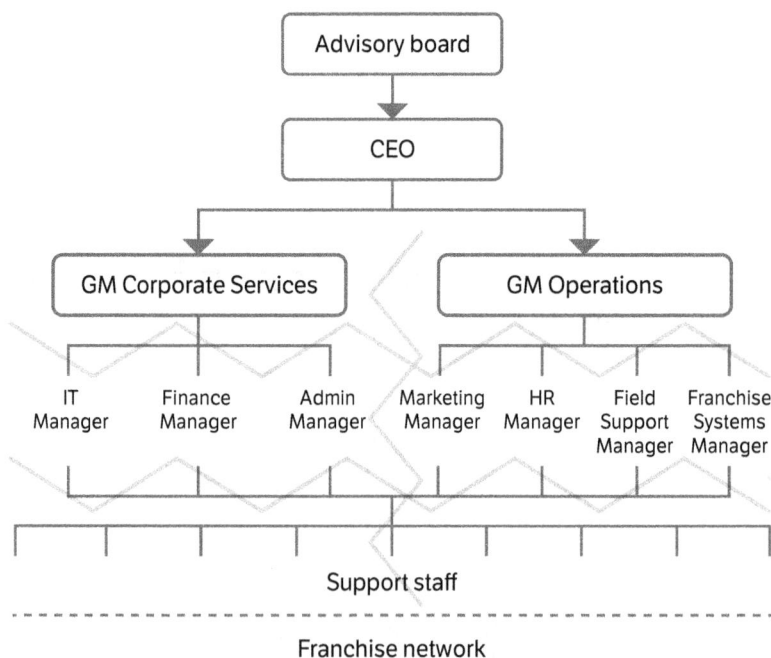

Self-destruction

The implosion came. It was inevitable, really – even a good thing, perhaps.

It seemed to me that the best way to move forward and redeem ourselves was to concede our brokenness. It needed to become our cause for change. In various team meetings I started to address the issues as I saw them. I was careful, but direct. I put words to what everybody else was feeling. I aired the ugliness.

People accepted that our current team shape and *modus operandi* was dysfunctional. They recognised we had resorted to self-preservation, a mere shadow of true team spirit, where self-interest superseded loyalty. They felt unsafe and afraid of what might happen if they exposed themselves in any way. They pulled away from the team dynamic and focused on their own work.

This led to a loss of agility in strategic projects and duplication of effort. Few people had visibility of each other's contributions. We weren't sharing the workload or the challenges. We became grossly inefficient. Projects took longer, and the results became substandard.

Further to this, because constructive communication was at an all-time low, few felt confident to share their career aspirations or progress along developmental pathways. It wasn't an environment conducive to learning or mentorship. Professional development and personal growth fell away. At its worst, we were stifling talent in people who no longer were prepared to take a risk and offer their knowledge or skills.

In a world where people are not working in an open and collaborative way, we resort to greater management controls. How else is the organisation to synthesise information and skills? The structure must prevail. It squeezed tighter as the commitment got looser. More frequent reporting cycles were imposed. Feeble attempts at control demanded pre-approval before action. The temptation to publish unyielding policies was hard to resist.

All this feeds the beast. People trust less. They think less. Results become bottlenecked. It creates a vicious cycle of *over*-management and *under*-leadership. We needed the opposite. People needed to *over*-lead and *under*-manage – me especially.

What once worked was now broken. In a short amount of time, we had gone from a high performing team breaking new ground and setting industry records to now feeling estranged from each other. Our structure hadn't changed on paper, but our culture had in the corridors. We were not having fun anymore. Going to the office was hard work, almost soul-destroying.

If everyone else wasn't considering new employment, I certainly was. I felt an enormous sense of disappointment, betrayal, and despair.

How did we get here?

More importantly, how were we going to climb out of this black hole?

Undoubtedly, this was the hardest season of my professional life.

Our structure and behaviour were distorting our aspirational identity. It simply wasn't working anymore. We became a victim of our own success.

At one time our structure had facilitated strong lines of communication and productive workflow. Now, it was being abused to justify selfish behaviour. I needed to change our structure to influence our behaviour. It was time.

The invitation

Jumping forward again to the morning that started with a limousine ride, the team were now gathered at the seclusive chateau.

With shoes polished and standing in full tuxedo, I cast the vision for a fresh approach to the way we could work together. Our new goal of 7/50/100 demanded that something must change. Our cultural dysfunction demanded the same.

I affirmed my commitment to each one of them.

I shared with them the learnings of my time since returning from long service leave.

I had spent the last few weeks meeting with every staff member individually. I had asked them what their aspirations were; what they felt their best contribution to the team was (or *could* be); what they observed to be the limitations we were facing collectively; and what they would change if given the opportunity.

In short, I was curious if they had faltered or flourished in our hierarchical structure. It was a loaded question.

I synthesised all these conversations. I concluded we had enormous untapped capabilities within our people and had outgrown our management structure.

I was optimistic. A new organisational model could create a better way of life. Delivered well, it would unearth dormant talent and restore dignity within our team. We needed to direct some sunlight onto the human seedlings that were currently starved for opportunity to grow.

I referred to us that day as a team *under development* – not fully mature like we may have previously been perceived; not Australia's best, like our brand suggested; not invincible or beyond reproach. We were starting again in some respects.

I reset the clock on the fundamental pillars of our team culture. Our new shape and structure had to suit the outrageous assignment of 7/50/100. I wanted to squash a style of dysfunctional autocratic management and unleash a new era of life-giving leadership. And I wanted them all to come on the journey with me, rather than be replaced.

I urged the team to help reset the norm with me – make something new together. Take baby steps if necessary, but move forward in the right direction. I wanted willingness to change. So I invited them to *join me.*

I didn't take for granted that everyone in the boardroom that day wanted to keep their jobs. I didn't assume they would buy into the new management regime and the story of 7/50/100 I was narrating. For some, I thought, it might be too much to ask; a reach too far. So I gave them all a choice.

The offer to retreat with dignity was extended. They could back away from the table with my full support, and be released for a new adventure elsewhere – no foul, no hard feelings.

But if they chose to stay, they must be committed to change – *real* change, change that I couldn't yet fully articulate. Those who remained were going to have to create something new together.

As of that day, the Back In Motion Health Group was put under *new management*. Or new *leadership*, to be exact.

They all signed up! At least, at first…

Brenda's story

What I remember most from the day in the limo was being *invited* to go on the 7/50/100 journey. Instantly different to any other meeting, strategy, or project I had been involved in as an employee – I was being invited, requested, asked to give my commitment to achieving this goal.

This was not at all a feature of traditional corporate life – here was a leader, standing in front of us, exposing his vulnerabilities, telling us he couldn't do it without us.

He didn't have to *ask*, he could have just *told*.

For many of us, that was the first time we saw the true heart of the *actual* leader of Back In Motion. Before that we rarely had access to the man, and any access was filtered through layers of hierarchy that ultimately diluted his capacity, impact, and personal influence.

In that moment, Jason broke down all the barriers, connected with us personally, and asked us to decide if we would join him. It was a powerful and unforgettable moment.

I took two weeks to give my RSVP to the official invitation, as the act of being invited impacted me so seriously. If he was willing to humble himself to our level, then I wanted to make sure I was prepared to honour my commitment.

Of course, I said "yes"!

Transferable Principles

6 The best form of leadership is *truth*.

7 Without *progressive change*, you may become a victim of your own success.

8 Teams thrive on *over*-leadership and *under*-management.

9 *Invite* people into change, rather than *demand* it from them.

3. COLLABORATION

The 'co'

For the first time in months, some faith was restored. The team crawled back into meaningful dialogue. We admitted our faults. We exchanged forgiveness. We identified that we all actually desired the *same thing*.

We made a vow of collaboration – where the 'co' reminded us we were in this together. In unity, we could aggregate our efforts. Collaboration was to become multiplication; leverage of our time, money, skills, experience and emotional energy.

And so began our search for a more congruent organisational model to overcome our cultural dysfunctions and spearhead the achievement of 7/50/100.

I took time to explore our options.

I continued to meet with individuals and small cross-sections of the national team. I wanted to extract the nuances they envisioned in our future organisational structure. I kept copious notes. I cross-pollinated each new conversation with the ideas and insights that I collected along the way.

We started to build some momentum. Like a geyser of steam pushing up through the earth's dry crust, eventually we erupted with creativity. People had a licence to muse *outside the box*. We granted everyone the freedom to think like mavericks – street fighters, even.

It was *our* business, and we realised we could manage and organise it any way we liked. We were still small and nimble, so the prerogative lay with us. Sensing an avalanche of change and a radical new approach, people leaned in. They all had an opinion. Energy levels rose. Optimism flowed. We hadn't produced anything particularly new yet, but the team was re-orientating with fresh eyes on the prize.

In his *One Minute Manager* series, famed leadership guru Ken Blanchard describes the four stages of team development as *forming, storming, norming* and *performing*. We had done a few laps of this cycle over the decade. With each revolution, we grew stronger and more mature.

After a sustained season of high performance, we now found ourselves once again *re-forming*, starting over again. This time, with the rich experiences of where we got it wrong with our complacency.

My leadership scorecard

I wasn't unaccustomed or afraid to lead.

For years I have been a devout student of classic and contemporary leadership literature. I was open to what new lessons I needed to learn.

In my late teens I had assumed primary responsibility for over 100 youth and 30 adult leaders as part of a local church community. This early experience became a springboard of confidence for me to take on various formal leadership roles during my university years. Soon after, I invested time serving on charitable boards and committees within professional peak bodies.

It wasn't long until I assumed leadership within the commercial context; namely, in my own business.

I stay current with as many popular leadership titles as I can read. I attend seminars given by the leading authorities on the subject.

And I have been rigorously mentored by other accomplished leaders for 20 consecutive years.

In my first five years of business start-up I even wrote a 12-month leadership masterclass curriculum that eventually become the seedbed for establishing the Iceberg Leadership Institute. Through this venture I have equipped hundreds of emerging and experienced leaders. I regularly give popular keynote presentations. I host a dozen two- and four-day interactive workshops each year. I present at seminars and conferences, write blogs and articles, and mentor individuals.

The Institute exists to encourage people to live with conviction, to have greater personal and professional influence in the world around them.

With all this in context, you could say I am a leadership enthusiast. Most would regard my natural leadership style to be an unpredictable mix of democratic tendencies with authoritative overrides.

I realised early in my career that I needed the contribution of others in a well-balanced team to achieve results. I willingly concede the lead to others when they demonstrate the requisite skills or knowledge. But I quickly assume responsibility when chaos or crisis prevails.

I find it easy to be warm toward people. I recognise their personal value beyond the workplace contract. In many ways, I see the contributions people make to any project as *their gift* to the cause, rather than an obligation they must fulfil.

Naturally averse to confrontation, I have intentionally developed over the years a refined skill of addressing uncomfortable and awkward matters with people in a way that demonstrates compassion without compromise.

I also routinely try to find some fun in the busyness of the race. I readily break character as the executive with what I, at least, think are funny antics or humorous games.

But it's not all good. There is a serious and sometimes dark side to my leadership.

I am demanding and tough when the stakes are high and the time is short. When under pressure and not at my best, I become very task-orientated and unreasonable in my expectations. Perfectionism and intolerance for mistakes are attributes I have to consciously guard against.

I am judgemental and critical by nature. I can overlook the nine achievements, and focus too heavily on the one disappointment. I also feel a rising impatience with people as I grow older. And I have little tolerance for laziness, shortcuts, and indifference.

And I can't deny the strong justice streak in me. While often serving the greater good, this has disabled my better judgement on many occasions. It makes me defensive – of self or others. It can express itself as militant aggression for whatever cause I'm fighting. And it can bruise people I care about.

I find myself being unnecessarily verbose at times; worried far too much about what others think of me; and narcissistic on my worst days.

So, like most, I am a *leader-in-the-making*. Jekyll and Hyde wrestling for position in any given moment.

This was the leadership style I modelled for 10 years at Back In Motion – for good and for bad. I was far from perfect in my leadership expression, but not ineffective.

Leadership crisis

Now, here I was facing some leadership demons. Admittedly, not for the first time. But never to this magnitude. A lot rested on my shoulders. At times, my determination was overshadowed by self-doubt.

Despite the turning of the cultural tide, the team was not safe yet. We were still stuck in the rip, albeit now purposeful in finding a way out. I needed to stay alert to avoid a false start or early slip.

And in my state, this wasn't easy. I was exhausted from the near-death team experience. We may have been moving in the right direction now, but at a price. I was worn down, frustrated, confused. And if I wasn't careful to internally manage my fragile inner state, I could jeopardise the new-found team enthusiasm.

This season in our business was for me an intense period of personal reflection and self-critique.

What had I done wrong?

Why didn't I see this implosion coming?

With hindsight, did I miss obvious warning signs evident in my managers?

How was my leadership deficient?

As we taxied down the runway of inevitable change, I drew heavily on our calling toward 7/50/100 as my aviation fuel.

Ownership myth

Change was being demanded from everyone.

We shone light into every dark corner of our team structure and organisational model. Rubbish bins were knocked over and rats scurried. In some cases, we found buried treasure that was worth keeping. In most cases, we needed to just keep moving on. We were cleaning house.

Nobody could hide. Especially me. In every respect, I had the most to lose and the greatest to gain. As the owner, this wasn't lost on me at any point.

In hindsight, I am grateful for not mistaking my ownership for leadership. That is, as the proprietor of a steadily growing organisation, with an increasingly more formal management structure beneath me and less hands-on involvement in the tactical workflow of the business, I could have fooled myself into believing few relied on me any longer for leadership.

Nothing could be further from the truth. My experience is that as operational visibility and daily responsibilities *decrease*, leadership presence must *increase*. That is, the less I *do* in the regular operations of the business, the more important it is for me *to be* someone of positive and powerful influence.

Of course, this is not to suggest that leadership attributes are not essential to effective management – on the contrary. But it is true that with less visibility and a less functional role within the organisation, the DNA of the founder or owner is at risk of mutation, or even extinction.

Staff may conclude by inference that an owner's increasing workplace absence is evidence of their dwindling commitment to the cause – maybe even indifference. For these reasons, organisational growth might work against you. Exponential leverage can have counter-productive credentials in the context of workplace relations.

Regardless, ownership should never be perceived as leadership. Don't confuse them. It's an illegitimate proxy. Just because someone holds equity or a controlling interest in the board, that does not equate to them having the attributes that inspire followership of the masses. These are different dimensions of authority and not to be mistaken.

I needed to step up in a new way. Even if I had at some point in the past, this was not a time to abdicate leadership now.

There was no comfort in the scale of our operations. Leverage depicted on an organisational chart was theoretical at this point. I needed to model a new and more potent form of personal influence. It was demanded of me. My position description was re-scripted – even turned *outside-in* and *downside-up*.

Innovative leadership become my primary objective.

Wish list

As the team mused on all the possibilities of a more effective and values-aligned organisational model, some themes converged.

We wanted the following attributes as non-negotiable features in the new workplace design.

1. Be less task-driven

Many had observed that their task lists were overwhelmingly long. Some suffered project fatigue. In our ambitious desire for *more* and *better*, we were burning out some of our brightest lights.

As previously acknowledged, I am by nature a very task- and work-driven leader. And of course, I reproduce after my own kind. I either recruit people like me, or mould them after the fact. This breeds more of the same. We created a culture of extreme work ethic evidenced by compressed workloads.

A strong internal drive to achieve was not inherently a bad thing. But it had to be tempered. It left very little margin for other considerations. And not all *activity* leads to *accomplishment*.

Every strength has a dark side in its extreme. When we became too task-focused we drove people into distress. This couldn't continue.

We aspired for a more holistic management approach. We wanted to emphasise relationships. Promote improvisation. Foster innovation and creativity in equal measure, to round out our task tendencies.

We believed we could do *better* by doing *less*.

2. Greater individual empowerment

For others to step forward, some of us needed to step back. For some to own their roles, others had to give up some rights. Managers needed to do less managing and workers needed to do more work. We declared zero tolerance for micromanagement.

The team could accept their mandate for organisational strategy and objectives, but wanted individuals to decide the tasks that were required to achieve the outcomes. This approach would bestow more freedoms. It would let people set their own priorities and work pace, without forfeiting accountability around results. It would enable creative expression and independent thought.

The ivory tower was besieged. The walls of bureaucracy had to come down. Those who were closest to the action needed greater authority to pull the right levers to effect appropriate change. Rather than tasks being dictated downstream, the team wanted to co-create their work agenda. This promised a more agile process through de-centralised decision making.

With 7/50/100 as the ultimate goal, individuals wanted to be trusted to explore what their best contribution to the team could be. Even if it wasn't on their current job description – even if it didn't fit into the current organisational chart.

Top-down pressure had to reduce. Individual accountability needed to increase. This was going to promote greater personal growth and organisational opportunity.

3. More free speech

The shy and quiet team members were withholding their valuable opinions from their peers. The dominant among us sometimes created unhelpful noise. Most of the time it was the same voices being heard. More people needed to speak up.

Balance, volume, and frequency mattered.

If people *think* it, they will eventually *act* it. So why not *speak* it? The brass needed to grant permission for people to speak freely. It had to become a standing order without fear of retribution.

I wanted to hear more ideas and contributions bubble through the structure. Opinions were to be shared. All votes had to be counted.

To impose less workload through the traditional lines of reporting, we needed more open dialogue and rigorous conversation flowing upstream. We imagined multi-directional lines of candid communication that transected the vertical hierarchical flow of the organisational tree.

4. New performance assessment

If we were to behave differently, then we should be assessed differently. Standards and expectations had to be reset. Methods of historic performance review and key performance indicators had to be discarded.

People didn't want to be measured and evaluated by a few people at the top. They opted for a regime where their *process* became as important as their *results*. The opinions and observations of their peers had to count for as much as those of their supervisors. And the supportive contribution someone might make to another's overall result should not be overlooked in an otherwise overly simplistic assessment.

Measures needed to be more holistic and values-based. People wanted to be rewarded for effort and results, and not just quantum of work-load. Completion of tasks had to include a qualitative grading.

Workplace motivations needed to be better understood. Bonuses and incentives had to be re-designed to facilitate true collaboration and strategic performance. We needed to avoid setting arbitrary deadlines for projects or work timeframes that distorted the quality or value of inputs.

Overall, performance should be rated as a team rather than a collection of individuals. We didn't want to promote lone wolfs or superstars. We wanted the team to be the hero.

We longed for a *champion team*, rather than a team of champions.

Our people decided that the traditional performance scorecard should be refined. It should be used to track high level trends and be visible at all levels of the new organisation.

Ultimately, we agreed that the mechanism for shared reward and performance evaluation must only be linked to those actions that accelerated us toward 7/50/100.

5. More intentional career development and succession planning

As a relatively small team with a short history, many people had yet to be given the opportunity to shine and flourish. People wanted more oxygen to breathe; headroom to grow; runway to take off from.

We made a shared commitment to work together in identifying new opportunities for anyone on the team who was feeling stale, under-utilised, or artificially pigeon-holed.

We needed flexibility in our role descriptions, and a willingness to take a risk with some people in exploring new horizons.

We were determined to hunt out some dormant passion, discover untapped potential, and accelerate young and emerging talent. In so doing, we would fortify the depth of our seedbed for future staff development and create reinforcement in key roles.

Those with determined and articulate ambitions were excited about the prospect of progression. The development of younger talent below and around them would create a rising tide for their own promotion – a groundswell of forward-moving people.

Research incubator

With the beginnings of our wish list coming together, we needed to find structural options.

A generous range of keywords were typed into online search engines. We spoke to peer franchisors and other organisations about their models. We bought books and downloaded relevant articles. I sketched multiple variations of our organisational chart on scrap paper at restaurants, in waiting rooms, and during the advertisements of late night TV shows. We drew on as many contacts and information sources as possible to ensure we had a thorough smorgasbord of alternatives.

I tended to incubate my thoughts on the running track or during long, hot showers on cold, lazy mornings. Others would wake up in the night, get distracted at their desk, or admit to a more bizarre creative bubble that worked for them.

As we collided in the corridors or wound up a meeting, we bounced off each other random suggestions and the latest insights from our independent discoveries.

I burned through a packet of multi-coloured highlighters as I marked up every journal, magazine article, textbook, or bestseller that in any way spoke value to our future form and function.

The clock was ticking. We felt pressure to reach a conclusion. But innovation can't be rushed.

The research into published case studies and innovative organisational models unearthed numerous alternatives. Through my reading I was introduced to the principles of adaptive change (Ron Heifetz), appreciative inquiry (David Cooperrider), holacracy (Brian J. Robertson), strength-based leadership (Marcus Buckingham), and requisite organisation (Elliott Jacques).

A long-lasting love affair with Kaplan and Norton's Balanced Scorecard, as taught by Harvard Business School, had always been a feature of our management ethos. We wondered how we could use it differently to effect greater change.

There were lots of options – and few clear answers. We were spoiled for choice and starved for clarity. Sometimes too many alternatives paralyse the decision. I definitely felt stuck.

Serendipity

Late one evening I received an online shout out from an absolute stranger. Someone who had read my blogs and picked up my twitter feed.

Jeremy Scrivens is described as a work futurist, a catalyst for innovation and collaboration. He is director of the Emotional Economy at Work – a consultancy that travels the world.

He connected with me online. He was intrigued with my journey and the random insights I was posting in 160 characters or less. The questions I was putting into the digital domain had him intrigued. Jeremy wanted to meet.

Our blind date lasted for two hours. To my delight, this new friend had some of the answers I needed. More importantly, Jeremy had a longer list of thoughtful questions that probed my thinking and intent.

He shared his experiences as an organisational consultant – the good, the bad and the ugly. He spoke of the historical context and *post*-post-modern world. He gave anecdotes, sketched drawings, and expressed cautions. He oscillated between high levels of animated energy, and quiet and curious observation.

The looks on his face were priceless as I shared some of my ideas. I couldn't tell whether his meal wasn't sitting well with him or it was my outrageous musings giving him trouble. He assured me of the latter.

Jeremy is a commercial centaur – part management theory and part risk-taking extremist. That's a good fit for me. I was fascinated by him… and excited for Back In Motion.

Naturally, we met a few more times. We ate more lunches, drank more tea, sketched more diagrams, and probed new possibilities.

With each conversation I felt like we were getting closer to the mark. The steps weren't objectively measurable each time, but the picture on the front of the puzzle box was starting to form.

Outsourced help

In the meantime, the team had talked, debated, brainstormed, white-boarded, and exhausted their reserves. We had creative block. A few were feeling dizzy from going around in circles.

All the shelf products lacked a certain something. Of course, they also each had a little something too.

Our cut and paste of the best of all worlds was creating quite an organisational mosaic. Our theoretical management structure resembled a year book collage of everyone's highlights and wish lists – but with no real spine or binding glue to hold it all together. It seemed right at this point to bring in an outsider to help navigate the process.

Enter Jeremy Scrivens; my quasi-consultant.

It was refreshing to have someone new to direct the conversation. Jeremy hosted some half-day engagements that sought to draw out of us the common threads of our ideal new world. He played the devil's advocate at times to challenge our ideas, and played the eternal optimist on other points when he wanted us to go further with an insight.

True to form with all consultants, we did the obligatory small group discussions, butcher's paper outlines, blue sky dream-building exercises, and psychometric profiling.

One of the greatest discoveries was looking at our team's spread of competencies and passions on an integrated profile. One complex chart empirically framed our overall strengths and deficiencies, immediately revealing the opportunity for holistic team growth.

A memorable moment in one of our sessions was the brave question of one doubtful team member.

"From all your experience in seeing how other organisations do things, can our ideas actually work?"

A curious look and wry smile slowly rippled across Jeremy's face. He answered:

"To be honest, I've never seen anything like this. It's radical and most wouldn't try it. But just imagine if it did work!"

Depending on whether your glass was half full or half empty that day, you heard something different. Some almost froze with fear because we were so far off the reservation. Most channelled the energy of possibility like a human lightning rod.

We were charged up and ready to call it.

Blueprint

The fundamentals crystallised. It was clear what we needed to do. In principle, we agreed to the following.

1. Vertical hierarchy had to be dismantled

We all agreed the pyramid was an unnecessary barrier to agile leadership and innovative thinking. At best, we bottlenecked creativity and responsive action. At worst, people could abuse others because of their ranking on a chart. Positions of authority were to be replaced with platforms of influence.

Instead of one-directional lines of reporting we favoured multi-dimensional peer accountability. Flattening it was an over-simplification. And inverting the pyramid just replaced one hierarchy with another. We needed to go three-dimensional and circular!

2. Titles needed to be stripped

In the same way people relied on hierarchy, titles had become proxy credentials.

Director. Executive Team Leader. General Manager. Senior Staff.

The problem is, titles are often ambiguous, incomplete, and self-limiting. Workplace titles are just words. Words can carry enormous power, or, if misunderstood, be entirely powerless.

Titles put people in category boxes. For us they implied more what people *couldn't* do than what they *should* do. We needed greater possibilities.

In our brave new approach, people would have meaningful and dynamic work descriptions. This would create white space for them to step into. They would say what was meant and mean what was said. It would be simpler, minimalist.

And descriptions could change – as often as needed for the person to make their *best contribution*.

Overnight, some people were going to lose their precious workplace identity. Most were going to discover an entirely more colourful one.

3. Team meetings needed to be re-scripted

Board, executive team, senior staff, and departmental meetings had overruled our schedule. They created division, not unity. The agendas were moot, or worse, often conflicted.

We published *minutes*, but wasted *hours*.

Meetings could no longer be the arena for posturing, politics, or game play. If we needed to meet, we wanted the right people in the room who could make a difference.

With no hierarchy and no titles, the guest list was open. If you had a reason to be part of the conversation, then no invitation was necessary. If the agenda didn't concern you, you didn't come.

Meetings had to produce action. Actions had to be accountable. Doors were to be taken off their hinges, as there was no secret business to conduct behind them anymore.

4. We wanted one team

In a small national leadership team of 25 people we had at least five competing ghettos of interest. Figure 2.3 showed this graphically. Vertically, we had tensions between the executive team, senior managers, and the support staff. Horizontally, we had the Operations team warring against Corporate Services.

Limited resources became the cause of civil war. Unity was long gone. We were living up to the namesake of corporate *divisions*.

It had to stop.

We all shared the same business model, the same clients to service, and the same aspiration. Simply put, we needed to break down the silos, defuse the turf wars, and re-band as one team.

Multiple functions – different skills – unique contributions: but *one* team.

5. Fairness had to be restored

Our workplace had become inequitable. Those empowered with titled positions grew in authority. Support staff and middle managers suffocated. Opportunity and professional development was sucked out of the room for many.

The rich got richer, and the poor got poorer.

The unfairness cut both ways. Bigger bonuses were paid to the executive on the backs of the teams that did most of the work. And junior staff avoided consequences when they failed in their responsibilities, while supervisors took the heat.

Not to be confused with *equality*, we wanted *equity*. Not *sameness*, but *fairness*.

Rewards and acknowledgement should flow to those who genuinely achieved. Penalties and consequences must be borne by those who missed the mark. We wanted a true meritocracy. People's efforts needed to be genuinely recognised, and not lost in the vast grey of ambiguity.

We also wanted the collective results to be celebrated by everyone. A true team identity promotes inter-dependency and community – each one doing their part. One sows the seed, another waters it, and a third harvests.

We needed everyone. Synergy begets shared rewards. No heroes and no villains… just peer-driven achievement where individuals can trust their co-contribution will be fairly rewarded.

The structural blueprint for our new management model was finally drafted.

Michael's story

When I heard all this talk about changing our workplace model and being creative, I couldn't believe it. It sounded like window dressing. Mutton dressed up as lamb. I had certainly worked in places where they tweaked changes to culture here and there, restructured the team, and introduced new values statements. But this felt like an overreach. Too much change. I remember thinking, it's just too risky to upturn everything.

It was at our first anniversary of Jason having introduced many of these changes that it dawned on me this wasn't going away. He was serious. It wasn't a trial, or just talk. He really believed in what he was saying.

I remember thinking I'd better get on board.

From the moment I started trying, things came easier than I expected. Although, not necessarily easy! It's amazing what can happen when you open yourself to something. As a natural sceptic, I was one of the slowest adopters. But I'm also still here – one of the longest serving team members.

My honest reflection is that even with all the good intentions, a model like we have created will naturally unwind again if we are not careful. It has to be continuously reset, maintained, and held to account. Human nature doesn't tend to work this way... so it requires effort on our part. But the payoff is there.

Tent poles

Some wondered at first if it all sounded too loose. Without hierarchy, titles, obligatory meetings, and departments they were afraid that nothing would get done.

Critics or poorly informed observers of our developing model labelled it as a structure-*less* approach.

This is untrue. We weren't devolving into a jellyfish with a diffuse belly. We were shedding our restrictive exoskeleton for the freedom of a different shape.

We were favouring a new model; not abandoning the significance of structure.

Structure and order *per se* were not to blame for our implosion. It was behaviour *within a structure* that led to our sensational demise. People were hypnotised into serving the model rather than demanding the model to serve us.

Structure is not good or bad. Rather, it is executed rightly or wrongly.

Mission and agenda can help inform structure. But structure is not the enemy. It's simply the tent poles. Steel and scaffolding. Infrastructure. The way people behave within the structure determines the culture. And culture is king.

I fondly recall my first night as a young boy camping in the mountains. I had a traditional A-frame tent. One big pole stood in the centre of the floor and the canvas draped all around me. It strikes me now the inconvenience of having to arrange my bedding and backpack around this obtrusive pillar. The pole always seemed in the way.

I was grateful for its function, but frustrated with its position.

These days tents are more versatile. The internal centre poles have gone. New technology and creative design has led to the development of external flexible poles that wrap around the outside of the tent. They are infinitely stronger, lighter, adaptable to varied weather conditions, and easy to assemble. More than this, they don't get in the way. The entire floor of the tent can be utilised. There is greater movement permitted and functionality achieved.

Our new workplace structure simply took out the centre poles of hierarchy, titles, and meetings that got in the way of flow and function. We still wanted framework, just a smarter and more flexible one.

We wanted our poles on the outside. We needed a more flexible structure: *outside-in downside-up.*

Reasonable objections

We were just about there. A lot had been decided. Organisational diagrams had been drawn. And new meeting formats considered. Role descriptions were being drafted. Old habits were being checked. And potential energy was stored.

We were poised.

Just before we leaped off the bungy platform for an exhilarating drop, some needed to test the rope. Was the harness fastened? Had the security checks been done? Were the instructors qualified?

All dressed up and with somewhere to go, it was time to jump. The longer we waited, the more nervous people became.

The knees wobbled in the final moments. Some last objections surfaced.

What if it doesn't work?

Are we being foolish?

If we don't like it, can we go back to how things used to be?

Is that person really able to change?

Can I change?

All the reasons why our new structure might not work still haunted us. Our thinking was challenged. Fears were labelled. Different assumptions were called out... again.

Some individuals who instinctively felt they had more to lose than gain, looked ghostly white. I was one of them. We were taking a leap into the unknown in search of a better way. We didn't have anyone to lead us. We were on our own... no case studies – no proven model – no map.

The objections lingered, and some couldn't be resolved. We just had to accept them. There was reasonable risk if we moved forward. There was greater risk if we stayed still.

We hugged it out – metaphorically, for some, literally, for others. It was time to test our theory and idealism.

We agreed to be *responsibly* irresponsible.

Evolution and revolutions

Not all change looks the same. As I look back over the growth of our organisation I see two distinct patterns.

Some have been slow and subtle. Steady adaptation – tweaks of a dial and gentle pulls of a lever, with gradual results. Characterised by gentleness, these changes are careful to not disrupt other attributes that are in some way co-dependent. It's more about continuous improvement – metamorphosis, the slow burn, developmental creep.

Simply stated, this style of change is an **evolution**.

Then there is an entirely other form of change I have experienced. It's radical – fast paced, sometimes ruthless and indifferent to what-ever is in its path. We went *left* yesterday and we are going *right* today. The foot drops hard on the pedal as the G-force lurches you backwards. It's about acceleration, not acclimatisation; U-turns rather than sweeping bends. You are *in* or you are *out*. Late adopters miss this form of change. People sitting on the fence get injured in sensitive and private places. It happens quickly – step change. If your seat belt is not on as the car takes the corner at full speed, you may roll out the passenger door.

Simple stated, this style of change is a **revolution**.

Change was inevitable and we had two ways forward: would it be by evolution or revolution?

It's probably no surprise, but there was never really any choice. It had to be the latter. We had to cleave the old way of doing things and overnight take up the mantle of a whole new ethos.

We set our go-live date. Our leadership revolution would start *tomorrow*.

Transferable Principles

10 Collaboration is *multiplication*.

11 Don't confuse *ownership* with *leadership*.

12 As operational visibility and daily responsibilities *decrease*, leadership presence must *increase*.

13 Beware workplace titles – as they can often be *ambiguous*, *incomplete*, and *self-limiting*. Encourage *best contribution* instead.

14 Prefer platforms of *influence* over positions of *authority*.

15 If people *think* it, they will eventually *act* it. So, encourage free speech early and respectfully.

16 Don't confuse *equity* with equality. Value *fairness* over sameness.

17 Organisational structure is not *good* or *bad* – it's just executed *rightly* or *wrongly*.

18 Change can be led by *evolution* or *revolution* – choose carefully.

4. INNOVATION

Namesake

Welcome to ONEteam™.

This was the namesake of our new leadership model – aptly described, simply named.

We were united – together again – aligned and centred on the same objectives. A team in the true sense of the word. Thinking as ONE.

Christening over, we introduced our new baby to the franchisees and clinicians of the Back In Motion Health Group.

The launch of ONEteam™ marked the first day of a living ecosystem that would produce self-led, highly collaborative, and peer-accountable colleagues jointly committed to the same mission. We distributed authority across the face of the team and empowered people to make their best contributions.

The genie was out of the bottle. The seal was broken. There was no turning back!

We started to think differently… talk differently… and eventually, act differently.

Office walls were literally pulled down. Desks got moved. People were given freedom to sit wherever it made sense to the relevance of their workflow. New clusters of creativity and productivity started to emerge. A bullpen was erected for open plan living. The commercial matadors stood ready.

Titles

Nobody lost their jobs – even if everybody lost their business titles.

Formal designations evaporated. Business cards were binned. And door and names plates were removed. Hereto forward, we agreed to simply refer to each other as *Colleagues* – the truest description to convey peer-ship.

Every member of ONEteam˜ was a Colleague. Every Colleague was a member of ONEteam˜.

Then came the dismantling of job descriptions.

If there was no need for contrived titles, then we had to also re-think the verbose corporate parlance that made up the proformas describing each job position. A Colleague's unique contribution was re-imagined into newly created Role Profiles.

We kept it real.

Each Colleague was empowered to author their own narrative of individual purpose in the life of the greater team.

People knew where each other stood… in some instances, for the first time.

Don's story

Coming from a traditional commercial background, I was very familiar and comfortable with hierarchy. When Jason announced the dismantling of our lines of report and organisational rigidity, I had real concerns about how I would be perceived inside and outside of the organisation. Truth is, I was really worried how a title-less position would look on my CV and LinkedIn profile, and how this would affect future job prospects when it was time to move on.

Losing my title was one of the first challenges to face. Ironically, it was also one of the quickest to overcome!

For me, qualifications and occupation were a big part of my personal identity. When I lost my formal workplace title, it came as a real challenge to my pride and perceptions of self. After some internal wrestling (and admittedly, hot debate with others), it came down to a fundamental choice. Was I going to let a title (or the lack of one) define who I was? Or was I prepared to ensure my behaviour and results defined my identity within the team?

It wasn't easy, but I was grateful when I let go of the title to grasp something much more fulfilling. Now, I don't think I care too much about titles at all.

A thousand words

Every revolution needs a symbol – an icon. Just like we see with Che Guevara, *Les Misérables*, Greenpeace, Catholicism, even Nike.

We needed one too. So we created our own.

Figure 4.1: Our logo

Our logo depicts an iconic planet with orbiting moons.

Why? Because despite conjecture, ONEteam˜ is not a flat structure. We also didn't just invert our pyramidal model, putting the client on top and the boss at the bottom. We didn't land on the contemporary platform of matrix management either.

Our organisation rounded out. It became three-dimensional in its expression. In the same way an orb has no top or bottom, ONEteam˜ became spherical.

A linear two-dimensional structural chart couldn't do justice to the ingenuity of our design. So we birthed something else. Something fun and playful. Something, we joked about, that was *alien* to everything we knew… strange and extraterrestrial.

We certainly weren't taking ourselves too seriously, but the idea felt like it was from another world!

To infinity and beyond

In our darkest months, we could feel ourselves been sucked into an organisational black hole.

As we resisted the negative effects of its gravitational pull, we were catapulted into new space – maybe even *outer* space… where no one's gone before. The galactic unknown, as they say in the classics. We were steering our ship toward the next frontier in workplace management.

Because the metaphor fit, ONEteam™ quickly became known as our *planetary* model of organisational leadership.

To infinity and beyond!

The adjacent colour bands in the planetary rim of our logo represent the many parts that make up an integrated whole. We were exploring a new way of working together. This picture spoke to our team *more* than a thousand words. It cast a vision for the story we were beginning.

Map of the stars

To navigate the unreached galaxies, we needed a map of the stars. We needed to plot coordinates into our navigation system to set trajectory. Without limits we might go too far. Worse still, we might be dragged backward into another black hole, despite our good intentions.

So we published a Governance Charter. It set out the structure, roles, responsibilities, policies, and processes of the ONEteam™ management system and leadership philosophy. It provided clear behavioural and performance expectations.

Twelve pages long, complete with a glossary of new terms and sub-headings for ease of reference, the Charter mattered. It was the rule book for a new game.

Planetary science

Astrophysics and stellar anatomy teach us lots about planets.

Firstly, they are made up of a core, mantle, and crust. Planets also spin on the axis of their own centre of gravity while orbiting the controlling influence of the sun within their solar system.

Many planets also have their own local moons circling in predictable paths, creating a complexity of moving bodies on the dancefloor of our heavens (see Figure 4.2).

Figure 4.2: Cross-section of planetary architecture

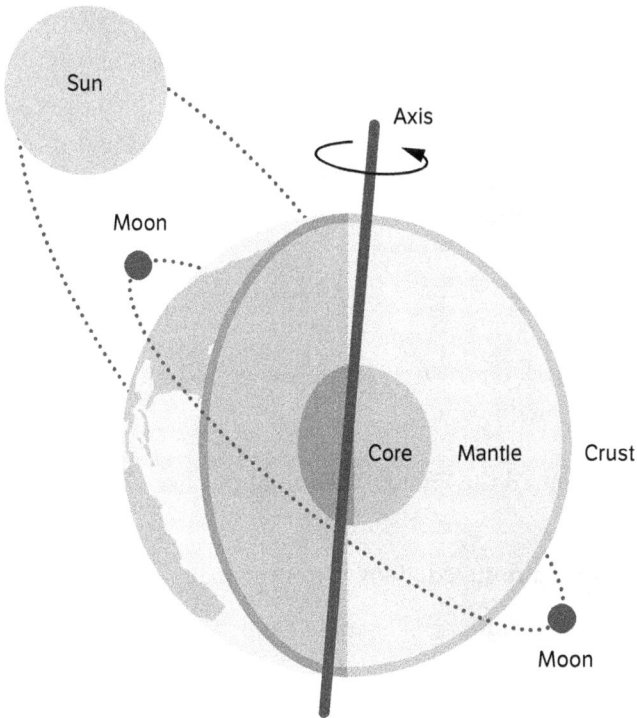

These planetary attributes can be shown more simply in the conceptual outline of Figure 4.3. This basic format became the blank canvas onto which we imagined our unique ONEteam™ future experiences.

Figure 4.3: Conceptual planetary model

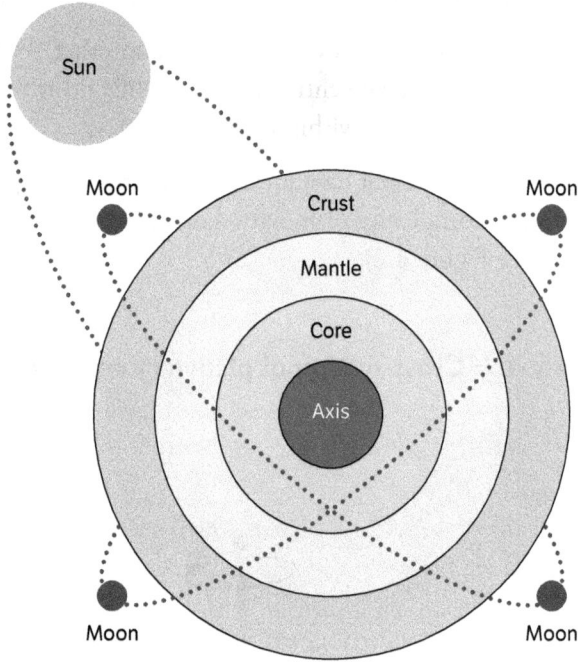

At a macro level, our new structure recognised some key elements of the planetary architecture:

- We recognised the **Primary Source** of our hope and motivation *(sun)*.

- We agreed a re-stated **Identity** to centre on *(axis)*.

- A **Strategic Target** or **Seasonal Theme** became our new focus *(core)*.

- A composite of specific skills and technical knowledge was organised into high performing sub-teams or **Functions** *(mantle)*.

- Supporting Colleagues called the **Support Ring** were committed to leadership, accountability, and strategy and encircled the whole team *(crust)*.

- Special-purpose executive responsibilities were then delegated to new configurations called **Pods** *(orbiting moons)*, to bring fresh influence on high stakes decisions and team direction.

Figure 4.4 translates the attributes of the planetary structure into the foundational elements of our ONEteam˜ organisational model.

Figure 4.4: Basic ONEteam˜ organisational model

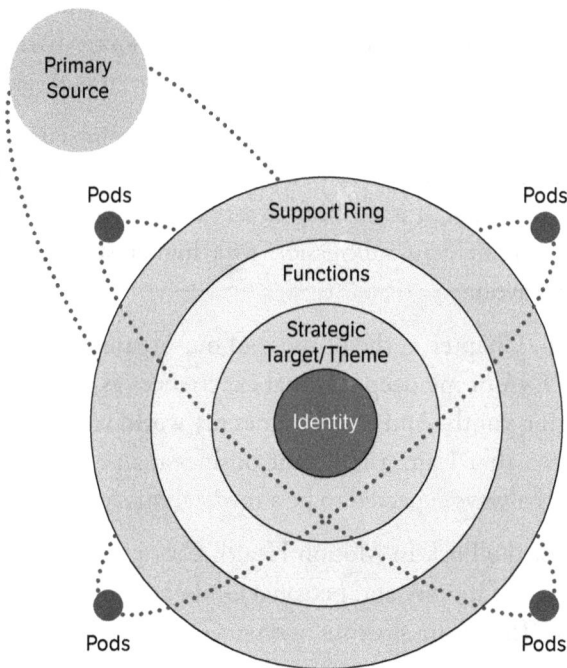

The sun

The sun has irresistible pull on the planets within its reach.

It's that big, bright, and shiny thing, way up high. You can't quite look straight at it, for fear of blindness. It's hard to describe. It gets hot when you're up close. And you know it's always there, even if you can't always see it.

Actually, the energy from the sun is the primary source of our planet's oxygen and food – of life, and of hope. In the same way, our organisational model relies on a Primary Source.

The sun of any workplace is the supreme influence that rests over the organisation. It could be a thought... an aspiration... a dream. It's often a cause much bigger than itself, such as a concern for the environment; a political ethos; or restoring dignity to marginalised communities. It might even be the self-absorbed ambitions of the owner or the board of directors in some corporate narratives. Or maybe it's the industry itself, with all of its external pulls and pushes.

In our instance, the sun is a set of deeply held spiritual convictions – biblical principles expressed in part by Judeo-Christian ethics. But even more than that, it is a calling to serve the purposes of God. Our organisation is held in submission to a higher standard than just human endeavour.

As shared in Chapter 1, the purpose of our organisation was seeded from the DNA of my deep spiritual experiences as a child, and then as a maturing youth. And it still frames my world view in adulthood. I share often that I am a reluctant businessman and an accidental franchisor. I always expected to be a medical missionary, not a CEO.

The plan for the Back In Motion Health Group was never really my own. A series of intense and personal God-encounters set my life on this course. The business exists to serve God's purposes.

I discovered early my dual calling to both empower people in optimal health, and serve the needs of the poor. They were defining moments for me. Unexplainable, but equally undeniable.

Gravity has its effects. So does the power of God. I can't resist either. Jesus Christ is the centre of my life… and so the *sun* of my organisation, my primary source of life and hope.

Even though I don't know what He looks like, I know His effects. The seasons of my life and business are ultimately under His influence – in constant orbit around God's intentions. This is true for me, and therefore true for the business I operate. Each one of us must recognise what sun is the centre of our solar system.

The axis

The earth rotates around its axis every 24-hour period. It pivots on its own centre of mass in perfect rhythm, entirely dependent on a geometric centre point.

ONEteam™ rotates on a precise centre too – this being its carefully defined *identity statements*.

The identity acronym presented in Chapter 1 remained as our organisation's axis.

MPV_1SV_2: Mission, Purpose, Vision, Strategy, Values.

Each one of these attributes must be clearly articulated.

Identity becomes the centre of gravity around which the entire workplace pivots daily. Don't be fooled into thinking this is a benign element of our workplace model. It's not new *thinking*… but it was new *doing*.

It's true, most companies have a mission statement. There's probably a plaque hanging in your boardroom or reception right now if you need to remind yourself. But how many live and die by them?

Back In Motion had always been a socially-conscious organisation. Our workplace had been values-driven and morally upright. We had cast vision and set strategic objectives every year to achieve results. We had published identity statements in all our annual reports and repeated them to audiences at key events.

It wasn't lip service. We really believed them. They were responsible for much of the cultural momentum we enjoyed as an organisation. In fact, they primed most of our success.

Putting up fresh identity statements now as part of our new team model was not in and of itself a dramatic shift from normal. It felt like an intuitive thing to do… familiar, obvious, maybe even expected.

That is, until we explained that MPV_1SV_2 was now the *axis* for ONEteam™:

- ▶ **Our mission** (what we do) is to empower clients in optimal lifelong health.

- ▶ **Our purpose** (why we exist) is to be significant to those in need.

- ▶ **Our vision** (where we see ourselves in the future) is to be the most loved and trusted provider of allied health services.

- ▶ **Our strategy** (how we will achieve our mission) is to provide effective leadership and comprehensive support to become the clinical provider, workplace, and business model of choice.

- ▶ **Our values** (the beliefs we are committed to) are excellence, leadership, loyalty, integrity, and significance.

At first, the profundity was lost on everyone. It probably sounded 'same, same…'.

But it wasn't the same. I needed them to acknowledge a fundamental shift. People no longer answered to Jason. Forget the owner. The axis had *replaced* me.

MPV_1SV_2 was made our centre point. Not just guiding statements, a north star, sentimental ethos, or expressions of idealism – the organisation was now to *entirely revolve around* these statements. Everything was to be measured and assessed relative to MPV_1SV_2.

It was our precise centre – our axis.

MPV_1SV_2 was now the boss. A new sheriff was in town. This became our accountability benchmark.

As the owner, I stepped aside. Trumped by a plaque on the wall. I willingly submitted myself to the authority and leadership as directed by our identity statements.

Colleagues were now invited to hold me to the same exacting standard of MPV_1SV_2. If any of my directives or opinions were contrary to these identity statements, MPV_1SV_2 rightfully overruled. I could be found wanting. No one was above it.

People were asked now to serve the *mission* as the master – not the *man* (see Figure 4.5).

Colleagues no longer had to wonder what the boss, manager, or supervisor thought about something. The guessing game was over. Everyone was empowered to assess their tasks, decisions, and strategic objectives based on the direct impact toward achieving MPV_1SV_2.

Figure 4.5: Serve the mission, not the man

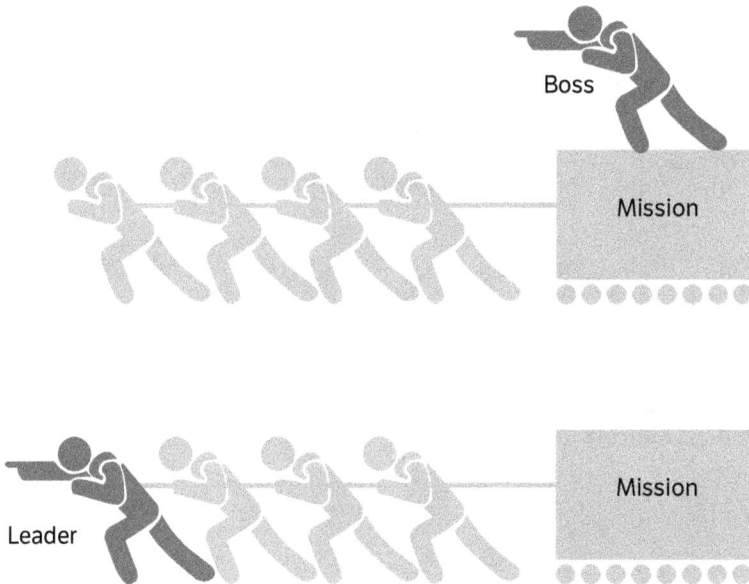

Embedded in our axis were the stakeholders closest to our heart. Namely, our:

- health clients

- practice workforce

- franchisees (practice directors).

They formed what I called our 3-legged stool. And it sat right at the centre of our new model.

We framed a clear strategy for each stakeholder. We committed ourselves to a shared focus on all three legs to keep our Identity in balance (see Figure 4.6).

Figure 4.6: The three-legged stool of our Identity *(axis)*

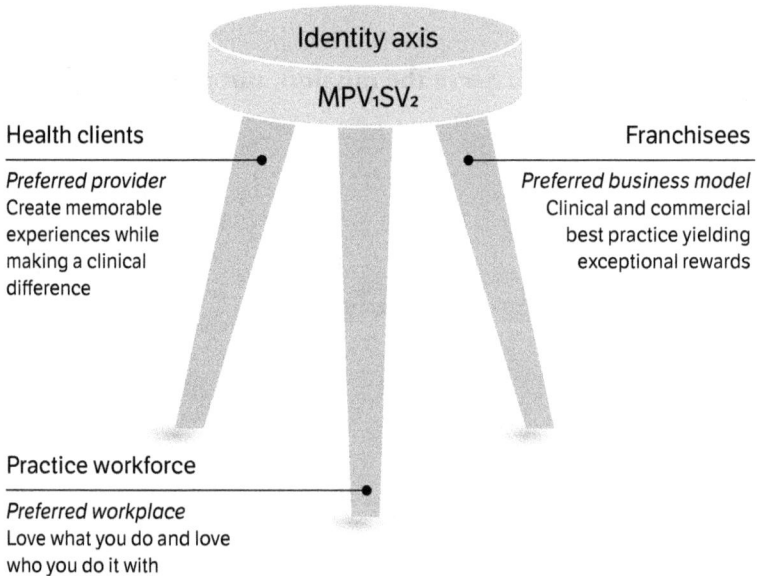

Identity axis

MPV_1SV_2

Health clients

Preferred provider
Create memorable
experiences while
making a clinical
difference

Franchisees

Preferred business model
Clinical and commercial
best practice yielding
exceptional rewards

Practice workforce

Preferred workplace
Love what you do and love
who you do it with

Not only did our national team submit themselves to the new reigning authority of MPV_1SV_2, but everyone we were here to serve got elevated. Our clients became the real heroes of our cause – rightly so. So did our staff, and especially our franchisees. This is why we existed.

They were the stakeholders we put right at the centre of our organisation – at the heart, in the bullseye. They become the pivot point on which we rotated our axis.

The prevailing ethos was bold. If the best interests of our clients, practice workforce, and franchisees were not central to every decision, task, project, and objective, then we had missed our calling.

This was not a case of the *customer always being right*. Rather we made it *right to always think of the customer*.

Every organisation has an axis. It's impossible not to. It could be the boss… or maybe profit, or peer awards, company policy, industry standards, or legislative requirements. The axis in some workplaces will be cultural axioms like 'self-preservation'; or maybe 'do as little as possible without being caught'; or simply 'work-to-eat'. Many organisations pivot on the sentiment of 'how things have always been done around here' – trapped in historical prisons of cultural apathy.

Whatever it is, the axis which lies at the heart of your organisation will become its point of greatest reference.

MPV_1SV_2 is our axis. What is yours? You have one. It's just a matter of whether you know it or not… and whether it's the one you want.

The core

The core of a planet is the dense material lying close to its centre – the hot, liquid fire. The axis rotates through the planet's centremost point of mass, but the core extends further.

In the ONEteam™ vernacular of organisational life, the Strategic Target (or Theme) represents our core.

A target is a goal. It's an objective. It's something to aim for. In its most simple form, it's a dream with a deadline. Necessarily, it's something realistically attainable.

Targets should be SMART (Specific, Measurable, Achievable, Relevant, and Timely). And where possible, even SMART*ER*, by ensuring they are also Ethical and Recorded.

Third only to the sun around which the organisation orbits, and the axis around which the team rotates, the Strategic Target is the next most central influence over Colleague behaviour. It's the operational compass – the strategic imperative for this season!

You must define the Strategic Target simply – in one word, or one sentence, or at least no more than one page. If it relies on a lengthy document, it's too complex. Strategic Targets must be highly memorable and transferable to every dark and forgotten corner of your workplace.

Organisations often lay down strategic plans in annual, three-year, or five-year periods. They are polished and presented. Catalogued and filed. Then quickly forgotten.

The strategy must be kept alive – every day. It mandates the core activity of the organisation. Each strategic plan must be distilled into one single key thought – a defining outcome – the main thing that must be achieved this season.

Targets for the strategy might be: internal growth; operational consolidation; product innovation; cultural enrichment; footprint scale; client diversification; or brand expansion.

Apple's target in the early 2000s was to lead the digital music revolution. Amazon's target is to be the most customer-centric company on earth – where you can buy anything online from them. Disney still wants to be the happiest place on earth, where dreams come true. Coca-Cola Amatil set a target to sell two of its related beverages on average to every adult in Australia per day. And Volvo has a target that no passengers in any of their vehicles will be killed or seriously injured after 2020.

Our Strategic Target during FY14–FY16 was 7/50/100. We set the aspiration to have our brand accessible in 7 states and territories of Australia, delivering $50 million worth of physiotherapy and related services, through 100 flagship practices.

This Strategic Target was core to our success. It was not more important than the sun we orbit, or the axis on which our team was centred. But it was the *next* most important.

Every Colleague within ONEteam" needed to know and understand the Strategic Target. For our people to become self-led, collaborative, and effective in their individual contributions, it was critical every action directly and positively moved the team closer to the goal. If not, they shouldn't do it. Peer accountability would remind them so.

The mantle

The bulk substance of a planet is known as its mantle. It's a mix of rock, water, soil, and gas. It represents 85% of the planetary mass, and so best defines the planet's attributes.

The mantle of ONEteam" is made up of skilled professionals, organised into sub-teams called Functions.

A Function is a specific domain of technical expertise and specialised knowledge that provides important organisational capability to ONEteam". As you can see in Figure 4.7 overleaf, Functions are interdependent wedges that converge toward the Strategic Target (core) and pivot on our Identity of MPV_1SV_2 (axis).

Six key Functions make up our mantle. Your organisation may opt for more, less, or just different ones. Our Functions are:

- Finance, Risk and Administration
- Network Development
- Practice Support and Performance
- Business Intelligence and Technology

- ▸ People and Systems

- ▸ Marketing and Communications.

Figure 4.7: The Functions *(mantle)*

Each Function has a clear and unique Mandate to achieve MPV_1SV_2. These Mandates are reviewed annually in July by the Functions themselves and endorsed by the broader team.

The *real* work of the business gets done in and between the Functions. The substance of organisational activity and workflow lives here. Projects, Taskforces, and Work Plans flow out of and into Functions.

We don't call our people in accounting the Finance *team*. If we did, in time it would become normal to also refer to our Marketing *team* and then our Technology *team*. Conceptually, this would already create three teams. Then what about the rest?

Our leadership philosophy is ONEteam˝. Not *THREE* team.

We have six specialised Functions, but we serve one mission. We are all fixed on the same axis. We are chasing a common Strategic Target. We are governed by a single Primary Source, the sun. Therefore, our structure reminds us to work as *one team*.

Each Function is made up of Colleagues with relevant technical and professional competencies to achieve their Mandate. Colleagues are not required to work exclusively for only one Function, but could make contributions in up to two or three depending on their skill sets.

Some Colleagues within each Function are invited to serve as Champions, Advocates, and Ambassadors based on their suitability for the role (see Figure 4.8).

Figure 4.8: The Champion, Advocate, and Ambassador of each Function *(mantle)*

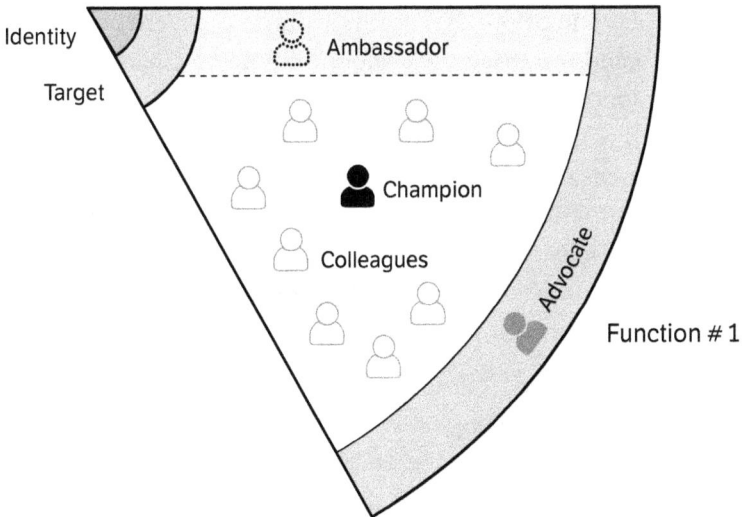

The Champion is considered captain of the Function.

They should not be misunderstood as the Function manager. ONEteam˘ doesn't have managers. We are a de-titled model of shared accountability and peer leadership.

In contrast to a traditional manager, the Champion is only responsible for:

- ► Overseeing the Work Plan;

- ► Approving administrative and financial requests where an individual Colleague has no delegated authority;

- ► Supporting the welfare of the Colleagues within the Function;

- ► Coordinating (but not unilaterally deciding) the recruitment and release of Colleagues from the Function; and

- ► Raising professional competency within the Function.

For example, one of our Colleagues with deep experience in other franchise brands accepted the responsibility to be Champion of the Practice Support and Performance Function for 12 months. This gave them the unique opportunity to set tone and culture within the Function; focus on the Work Plan; and lead from within. However, ONEteam˘ structure does not require the Champion to micro-manage all of the activities of each Function member. Conversely, each Colleague was individually responsible for their own objectives and performance within the Function.

After a year, another Colleague with suitable experience was given the opportunity to Champion the Function. There was no promotion or demotion – just a rotation. There is no fixed tenure or limit for how often this role may shift to share the load as necessary.

As evident in Figure 4.8, the Champion is certainly not *above* anyone else. They are part of the sub-team. They are playing captains on the field – responsible for their own contribution, but helping the players remain focused on what they can achieve together if they stay true to their agreed plan.

David's story

Hierarchy is a topic that is often misunderstood and hard to grasp at first. For me, it has been so hard to shake the 'top down mentality' as there is often a feeling of 'losing control' or not being valued for your position. The hardest part for me was accepting a role as Champion and trying to resist the urge to *manage* people. This took me many months of getting it wrong before I got it right.

The ability to switch from a manager's lens to that of a leader has been my single most difficult challenge. I had been used to positions of responsibility where I was required to make all of the decisions. Sharing this load with peers and Colleagues was a much harder shift than I had imagined. Nice in theory, but really hard to live.

But this impetus for change became my tipping point in the development of my true leadership. I slowly learned how to harness the best in people rather than just pick the bits I wanted from them or felt the organisation needed. As a result, I ended up with a collaborative Function that has learnt to voice their opinion, contribute to the broader business, and help bring a considered approach to complex problems. This not only gets us a better result, but it usually gets us there faster!

As I reflect on previous years, I can't honestly recall a time where we have been able to achieve so much in such a short time. Learning the difference between leading and managing has become a pivotal turning point in my career. The benefits of sharing reasonability have certainly outweighed the fear of losing control.

The Advocate is more like the coach to the Function.

They are not superiors, department heads, or executives. They sit alongside Colleagues rather than above them. Their opinions do not carry unilateral or superior authority over their peers.

By design, Advocates are non-technical Colleagues at arms-length to the tactical work of the Function. They serve as an effective sounding board and bring accountability to the Function Mandate.

Advocates are primarily responsible for:

- Giving objective perspective to the Function;
- Providing accountability to the Work Plan;
- Promoting cross-Function collaboration;
- Approving administrative and financial requests that are not covered by the Champion's Role Profile;
- Assisting in the recruitment and release of Colleagues from the Function; and
- Supporting the welfare of the Colleagues within the Function.

In one instance, a Colleague from our People and Systems Function served as the Advocate to the Marketing and Communications Function. They were not likely to speak to the specifics of a segmented social media campaign, but they could certainly bring value in assessing whether such activity was aligned to the Strategic Target of the whole team.

By not being too close to the work, the Advocate can be objective and critical. They can see the woods, even if they don't know the species of every tree.

Advocate responsibilities are not full time. They are regarded as Secondary Work Descriptions in a Colleague's Role Profile and constitute approximately only 5% to 10% of a Colleague's work time.

All Advocates, by definition, are appointed from outside the Function. This encourages cross-pollination of talent and broader organisational perspective. It imposes a degree of collaboration.

By design, every Function has within its working group, intimate links to other Functions. It makes silos and turf wars far less likely… in fact, almost impossible.

Functions also rely on Ambassadors.

Ambassadors are not permanent designations. They are temporary assignments – contextual deputisations – granted to the most appropriate Colleague to act on behalf of the Function for a specific task. That is, representatives for a defined purpose.

Ambassadors may take the lead on a Function Project; contribute to a cross-Function Taskforce; represent strategy at collective ONEteam˜ meetings; or even work with external stakeholders on behalf of the organisation.

Once the specific purpose has been fulfilled, the delegated authorities and responsibilities of the Ambassador cease. Different Colleagues may be appointed as Ambassadors to best act in other matters when they arise.

One of our newest and less experienced accountants in our Finance, Risk and Administration Function become the perfect choice to be an Ambassador in a technology transformation Project. While they were not the highest paid Colleague in the Function, and did not carry the Champion responsibilities, they did have past experience with another employer in similar projects. This Colleague was therefore identified as our best resource to lead the way, and represent the finance imperatives in the planning meetings and think tanks with other Functions.

During their appointed time, the Ambassador carries higher specific authority than anyone else in the Function – including the Champion and the Advocate. This delegation may only last two, four or six weeks, until the Project has moved on, at which point the Ambassador authorities are removed from the Colleague's Role Profile.

We see this same principle at work in foreign relations and international diplomacy. Ambassadors carry the authority of the President or Prime Minister, and at such time are empowered to make their best judgement on behalf of the nation they serve.

Conceivably, a Function may have more than a dozen demands on it at any time. All Colleagues within the Function may carry Ambassador responsibilities in different areas. It's our form of *concurrent leadership* – authority in parallel, but not in conflict.

The war cry of the ONEteam™ philosophy is cross-collaboration (see Figure 4.9). Functions are expected to work together, cross the floor, share ideas, and face one another. To challenge and provoke. Colleagues, Champions, Advocates, and Ambassadors make this happen.

Figure 4.9: Cross-Function Collaboration of Colleagues *(mantle)*

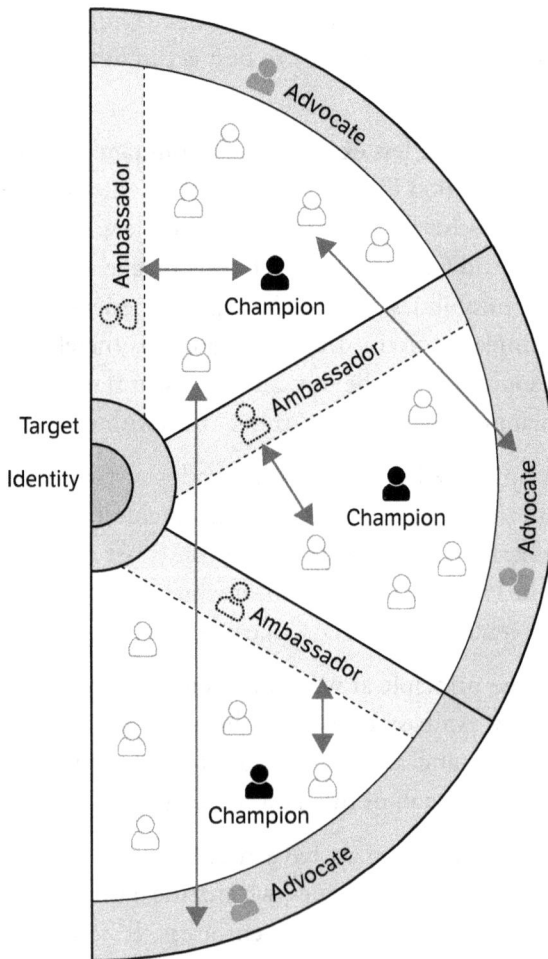

At the same time, a high-performing team must avoid negative group-think – as a whole, and within a Function. We must sense check our intentions with others, brainstorm in an open format, but never drink the local Kool-Aid.

Healthy levels of collaboration between all Colleagues across different Functions helps the best ideas to win.

The crust

The periphery of any planet is known as the crust. It's the outer surface that includes mountain ranges, ocean floors, and life as we know it. It sets the climate and displays the topography. It's the world we know and recognise.

In the ONEteam™ model, the crust is represented as our Support Ring.

The Mandate of the Support Ring is four-fold:

1. *Govern* ONEteam™.
2. Encourage cross-Function *collaboration*.
3. Provide holistic *accountability*.
4. Bring organisational *leadership*.

It is not directly operational. It does not provide specific technical expertise or specialised knowledge like a Function.

It supports, it enables, it empowers – but it should rarely *do*.

In place of Champions, Advocates and Ambassadors, the composition of the Support Ring includes an Executive Lead, Associate Leads, and Advisory Board members (see Figure 4.10 overleaf).

The Executive Lead is the Colleague invited by the Advisory Board to be the principal facilitator of ONEteam™. They are not the CEO, as no such title designation exists. They do not have unilateral controls. They cannot hire and fire on a whim. They do not set the rules of engagement. They can't change strategy without team consultation. They are *not* the boss.

They are best described as the *first among equals*, responsible for:

► Ensuring effective collaboration between the Functions and Pods;

► Approving ONEteam™ administrative and financial requests where no Function carries the appropriate authority;

► Liaising with the Advisory Board;

► Governance of the ONEteam™ Charter; and

► Progressive achievement of the Strategic Target and MPV_1SV_2.

Figure 4.10: The Composition of the Support Ring *(crust)*

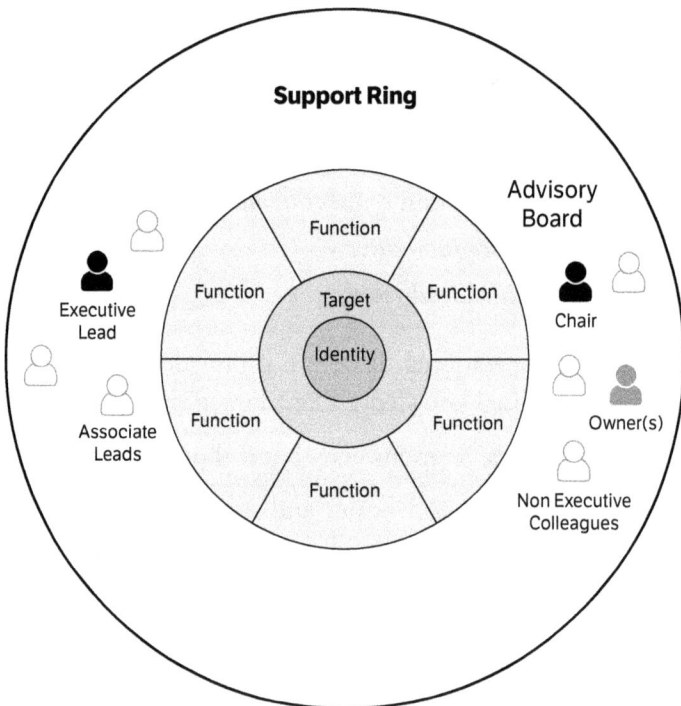

Frankly, the role can just feel too big for one person at times. So the Advisory Board may also invite additional Colleagues to fill the Role Profiles of Associate Leads.

An Associate Lead is a supporting facilitator of ONEteam™. They are responsible for assisting the Executive Lead with a specific portfolio delegated to them.

In typical fashion, the Colleagues who carry Lead Role Profiles (Executive or Associate Leads) do not belong to any one Function. They are universally engaged in cross-Function projects and collaboration Taskforces.

The Advisory Board is an external consulting body made up of the Owner(s), a Board Chair, and specially appointed non-executive Colleagues.

The Advisory Board are responsible for:

- Assigning and supporting the Executive Lead;

- Approving the appointment of Associate Leads;

- Providing objective and strategic insights to the Functions and Pods;

- Long-range organisational planning and capability; and

- Ultimate governance of MPV_1SV_2.

Non-executive Colleagues at the Advisory Board are appointed and released by the Owner(s).

The Owner(s) may appoint one of the non-executive Colleagues as the Board Chair, or an Owner may fulfil this role.

The Advisory Board is governed by its own Sub-Charter, to deal more specifically with its unique roles and responsibilities within ONEteam™.

The Owners are the Colleagues who literally hold shares in the organisation. They may simultaneously carry operational responsibilities under an employment framework, or simply be passive investors.

While equity and shareholding would typically imply an enormous amount of authority and control, in ONEteam™ the Owner(s) has very few direct responsibilities. They can't pull rank or trump. There are no 'owner's cards' to play.

In fact, the only delegated powers for the Owner(s) to carry out are the:

- Appointment of non-executive Colleagues and the Chair to the Advisory Board; and

- Approval of changes to the ONEteam™ Governance Charter.

Beyond these two individual responsibilities, the Owner(s) are fully replaced in any individual power-broking capacity. All other decisions, authorities, and activities have been delegated to the Advisory board, Support Ring, Pods, Functions, or Colleagues.

The Owner must *decrease* so the team can *increase*.

In traditional management, the board, CEO, and executive team retain full veto on any decision carried out across the organisation. In many cases, they live at the centre of the activity. Instructions flow from top to bottom. Permission is asked from below. Blessings are granted from above.

In our ONEteam™ model, all of these traditional C-suite roles are marginalised into the Support Ring. The Support Ring is peripheral to most of the real action. Those who perform closest to the core have the most influence over our key stakeholders and achievement of the Strategic Target.

Decision-making and authority is encouraged at the coalface. Colleagues with the capacity to best contribute to MPV_1SV_2 are typically those who fight on the front line – not the generals poring over a map and a theoretic battle plan in the safety of their bunker.

ONEteam™ is designed as a model of distributed authority and peer empowerment. It promotes freedom and responsibility. Relegation of the old-world management to the Support Ring is what makes the team agile. The effect is nimble service and outstanding results. Clients benefit. Targets are reached. Everybody wins.

The planetary model of ONEteam™ eliminates *lines of report*. We put *lines of support* in its place. Without managers and hierarchy, Colleagues must self-manage. If they need assistance, help is available. Where once people felt fear and intimidation from superiors, the model encourages mentoring and advice. The tables are turned.

We flipped the organisation inside out. Well, *outside-in* and *downside-up*.

The moons

Many planets have orbiting celestial bodies caught in their gravitational fields. We call these moons.

ONEteam™ calls them Pods. A Pod is a permanent special-purpose leadership group working on behalf of and orbiting ONEteam™.

There are two types of Pods: *Executive* ('Executive Pod') and *Ancillary* ('Pod').

The three **Executive Pods** designed for our purposes at Back In Motion were:

► **Strategy and Innovation** – where the strategic plan was reviewed; performance against the balanced scorecard was measured; and creative innovations were explored, debated, and commissioned.

► **People and Rewards** – where workplace culture was promoted; individual performance was evaluated; careers were planned and developed; and decisions regarding the recruitment and release of Colleagues was decided.

► **Stewardship** – where finance, budgets, and forecasts were monitored; investments into new ventures were assessed; and where efficiencies across the whole organisation could be optimised.

The two Ancillary Pods were:

- **Health-Pod** – where the physical and mental wellbeing of Colleagues was protected and promoted.
- **Fun-Pod** – where social agendas, team building exercises, and celebrations of achievements could be planned and executed.

As with the Functions and Support Ring, each Pod has a clear and unique Mandate to achieve MPV_1SV_2. The Mandates are reviewed annually by the Pods themselves and endorsed by the Executive Lead.

In addition to a Colleague's primary technical role, they may also be offered by the Executive Lead the opportunity to chair a Pod.

The Pod Chairperson is the principal facilitator of the Pod and is responsible for:

- Assigning and rotating Colleagues from different Functions within the Pod;
- Development of and accountability to the Pod Work Plan;
- Approving administrative and financial requests of the Pod;
- Raising professional competency within the Pod; and
- Promoting cross-Pod collaboration.

The Pods rely upon three to six Colleagues invited by the Pod Chairperson to achieve the Pod Mandate.

The composition of the Pod must represent a cross-section of ONEteam™. It should contain no more than two Colleagues from any one Function, and at least one Colleague from the Support Ring (see Figure 4.11). We prefer a mix of gender; diverse ages; different skill sets; and Colleagues of different tenure within the Back In Motion journey.

Figure 4.11: The Composition of the Pods *(moons)*

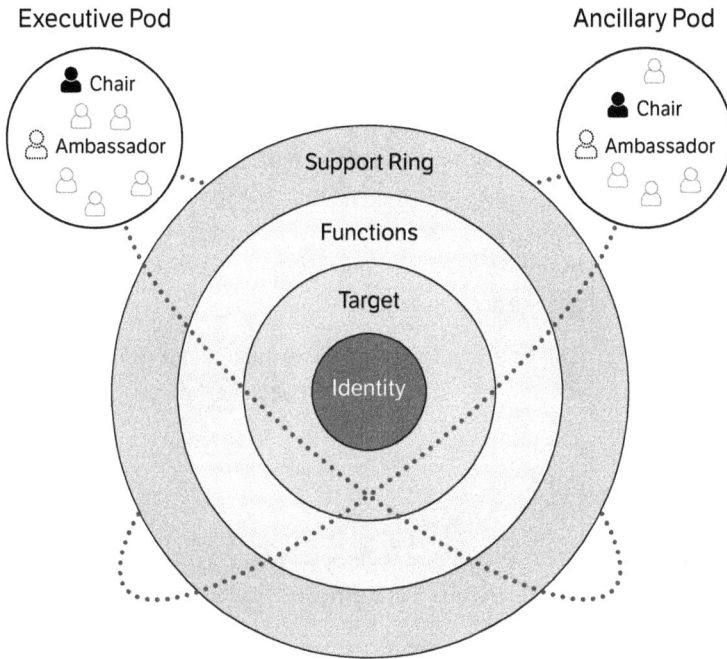

Caitlin's story

In all my previous roles I have experienced layers of predictable management hierarchy. So coming into my role at Back In Motion with their unique ONEteam™ structure certainly took some time getting used to.

However, after now having lived this new way of life for over four years, I think I'm ruined for the alternative. This innovative approach to working has been great for our business and culture.

Because of ONEteam™, it means I have been able to take responsibility for a part of our workflow that I'm sure ordinarily I would have been overlooked for. I would have been too young. Too inexperienced. Or simply, just too quiet. But in this workplace, everyone matters. So, I took on the role of chairing the Health Pod.

This meant that I had to learn how to convene meetings, put together a small budget, collate the views of the whole team on their preferences, and ultimately decide what was in our best interests with regards to being well in all aspects of team life.

I ended up arranging massages at our workstations, set up a small gymnasium onsite, instituted regular exercise breaks throughout the course of the day, put healthy snacks in the lunch room, arranged some mobile stand-up desks for those who wanted them, wrote a policy for pets-at-work, and championed the idea of walking meetings to keep us active. We even had a planking challenge at 11am every day.

Of course, it wasn't just me. I had a whole Pod to support me. But they needed a leader, and because of ONEteam™, I became that leader. How exciting for me!

Contribution to a Pod is listed as a Secondary Work Description in any participating Colleague's Role Profile.

The most appropriate Colleague to act on behalf of the Pod for a defined purpose is deemed to be the Pod Ambassador. This occurs in the same way an Ambassador of a Function carries a temporary delegated authority.

The big picture

The anatomy of ONEteam™ is certainly different.

It might look confusing at first... possibly strange... maybe even unnecessary. But it works.

ONEteam™ is planetary by nature. And when you put it all together, it looks something like what's shown in Figure 4.12.

We had re-imaged our organisational structure. Back In Motion was designed to orbit around the bright light of a Primary Source based on my spiritual convictions. We rotated on the Identity axis of our unique statements captured by MPV_1SV_2. We had at our core a clearly defined Target of 7/50/100 for the strategic season FY14–FY16. The mantle of our group was substantively made up of six converging technical Functions. The Support Ring wrapped around the periphery like the planet's crust. And we captured our special interest leadership groups in orbiting moons called Executive Pods and Ancillary Pods (see Figure 4.13 overleaf).

Figure 4.12: The complete anatomy of ONEteam™

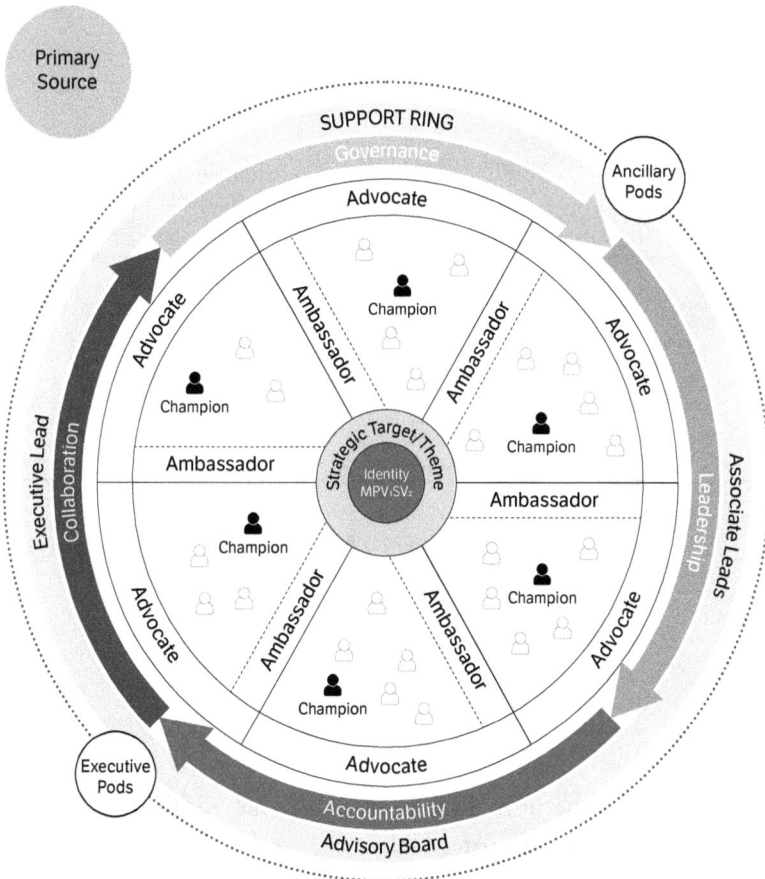

Figure 4.13: The Back In Motion iteration of ONEteam™ (FY14–FY16)

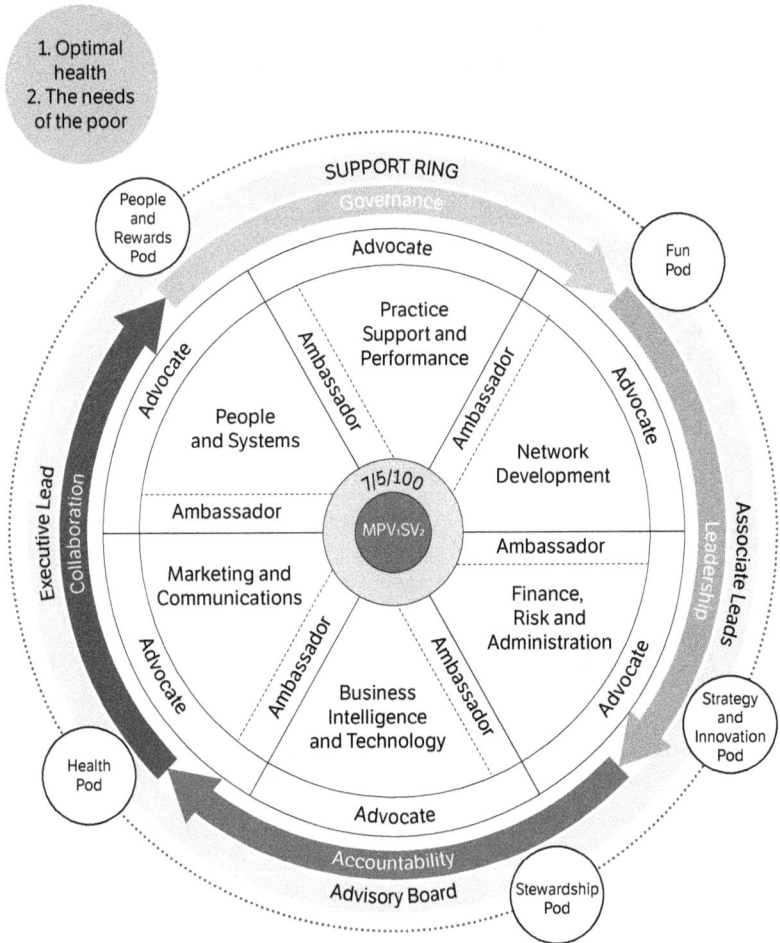

This was to be the next three years of our life within the Back In Motion Health Group… maybe longer.

It's a lot to consume in one chapter. It was more to undertake in real life.

Resist the urge to feel overwhelmed at this point. Remember, it wasn't an overnight change. It was months in the making. We didn't possess any standout qualities in our team that should make your workplace feel inferior. We simply proceeded with the predictable attributes of courage, creativity, and the often underestimated advantage that comes from desperation.

The big picture was clear, but the devil lay lurking in the detail.

Our structure was certain. The tent poles had been moved to the outside. An open plan style of decision-making and collaboration could now exist. *Outside-in.*

Clients were placed at the heart of our organisation. Managers had been decommissioned. Colleagues had been empowered. *Downside-up.*

All that remained was the right behaviour within the new structure. Could we really become ONEteam™? It relied on a little thing called *culture.*

The test was about to begin.

Transferable Principles

19 Every organisation has an *axis* of *identity* – just not necessarily the one they chose.

20 The manager must *decrease*, so the team can *increase*.

21 Serve an organisational *mission*; not a literal man or woman.

22 Distributed authority empowers *freedom* and *responsibility*.

5. CULTURE

Making a meal of it

So much has been written around the world on culture. There is a whole sub-culture even, on the topic of 'culture' in modern literature. Popular thinking and academic theories seek to make this subject matter the pre-eminent indicator of workplace success.

I think they are right!

Peter Drucker's oft-quoted axiom is that 'culture eats strategy for breakfast'. If this is true (and it probably is), then culture also ingests *vision* at lunchtime and devours *structure* for dinner.

It's simple. We had a new innovative model: ONEteam™. But culture still mattered. And it makes a meal of anything that attempts to substitute it.

Enjoy your articulate and inspiring vision. Boast a brilliant strategy. Rely on your innovative leadership structure. Point to your past successes. Revel in the demise of competitors to the left and right. The truth will prevail, though… a destructive culture will still bring your team to its knees.

Our work was clearly not finished.

The heart of the book

This book chronicles our workplace revolution. We turned ourselves *outside-in* and *downside-up*. Incremental change was going to be too slow to save us. We needed to lead differently, almost immediately. ONEteam˜ was new, whereas the old and stale was occupying valuable space.

But we couldn't stop at just the design of a new structure. In short, we had to re-create our culture too. Actually, this is what we had to do *mostly*.

This is the fifth chapter of nine in the book you hold. The binding stitches of the spine of this book literally run right through the middle of this topic. They should – this is not by accident. The culture challenge is my central theme of ONEteam˜. It's the heart of my message. Ignore culture and all your other efforts will be in vain.

Ours certainly were.

Don't simply rearrange the deck chairs on the Titanic. You can recast a vision; launch a new strategy; invent a different business model; and upturn your workplace structure. You will look fresh. Different. Even better… for a while. But if you leave culture unaddressed, the ship is still going to sink.

Seal the leaks in your hull. We reinforced our culture with titanium steel.

The air is thin at the top

Most leaders assume their culture is better than it really is. They see what they want to believe. Australian CEOs report that culture is talked about three times more often than it really is. They positively score culture more than double what their colleagues report (*EPIC Leading Workplace Cultures Survey Report*, April 2011).

Unknowingly, I was no different. As most C-suite executives did, I positively exaggerated our workplace culture. None of us were lying… just deceived. Optimism blinds reality.

The higher one climbs the workplace mountain, the less oxygen is available. When you reach the summit, the air is super thin. Cultural hallucinations prevail. You see things that aren't there. And miss the things that are!

Culture is best defined by the masses – not the leaders. The privileged few at the top have a distorted picture. Find out the experience of those at reception, in accounts payable, and on the sales team. Their view counts the most. What they think, see, do and feel *is* your culture.

Our team were telling me our culture didn't support the new ONEteam™ model. Fortunately, I listened.

We all have one

Every workplace has a culture – intentional or not, constructive or otherwise. You don't even have to plan for one. They just happen. Those who haven't invested into their culture will inherit one.

Every team gets the culture they deserve. If you have worked hard to positively frame the behaviours of your workplace, then congratulations. Commiserations to those who haven't.

With culture, there should be no surprises. For every action there is a consequence. If you are passive toward culture, you will still end up with one… just not the one you want.

Culture is shaped by the minutes and the moments. It morphs daily, although not in a day. You can lead your culture or follow the path of least resistance – but don't complain you weren't there! If you are not intentionally building a *specific* culture, then you are unintentionally building an *alternative* one.

Our team decided it was time to re-set.

Unwritten ground rules

So much could be written on the topic of culture. Fortunately, others have laboured in this area on our behalf, and so I won't. Discarding all sophistication, culture is quite simply *the way things get done*.

Culture isn't vague, nebulous, or grey. It's real and palpable. It's otherwise thought of as the *unwritten ground rules*. Culture becomes the personality of your team. It's shaped by the collective. It reveals who you all *really* are!

The culture wheel has many cogs, including:

- ► shared meanings and common interpretation of events
- ► perceptions
- ► preferences
- ► behavioural codes
- ► basic values
- ► myths and legends
- ► stories about the past
- ► heroes and villains
- ► emblems
- ► rituals.

Our culture was best depicted by repeated statements. People wanted to be safe. They wanted implicit support to do what they were best at. They wanted to enjoy the journey and not just the destination.

Authentic culture drives behaviour!

My eyes were wide open. I inherently knew that our unwritten ground rules would be more influential than any scripted messages or workplace posters about our new leadership approach.

We needed a fresh level of commitment. A constitution that governed our culture. A shared covenant.

Culture Commitment

Remember, a *happy* team is not always a *healthy* culture. The first is a short-term emotion; the latter is a long-term experience.

The Golden Rule exhorts us to treat one another as *you* would like to be treated. Not good enough! We opted for the Platinum Rule. Our promise was to treat each other as *they* wanted to be treated.

Through a series of detailed workshops, team meetings, staff surveys, reflective exercises, WIFLE (What I Feel Like Expressing) sessions, and individual interviews we drafted our ground rules.

It was exhausting. But very necessary!

We encouraged respectful disagreement, innovative thinking, and counter-views to extract real opinions. Never has the devil had so many advocates in one room!

Eventually we formed our Culture Commitment. Our matters of the heart that should influence how we play the game of ONEteam™. We stated it simply. Owned it collectively. Embraced it personally. Cast it convincingly. Repeated it regularly. And celebrated it sincerely.

It was a shared experience.

We determined to release more natural talent within the team through effective collaboration. Achieving our stated purpose was the ONEteam™ prize.

Our Culture Commitment demanded fresh courage – and trust, which is only earned when actions meet words. It centred on not just *doing* well, but *being* well. We agreed that what we achieved would be important, but how we behaved getting there, mattered more.

Pillars and Principles

Our Culture Commitment imagined a workplace of freedom that was centred on two Pillars. Yours may look different, but here's what we settled on.

► **Pillar One** was an expectation that all Colleagues would *fulfil their commitments.*

Each Colleague agreed to do what they said they were going to do, and take ownership as though it all came down to them.

► **Pillar Two** was an expectation to *lead naturally.*

Colleagues agreed to lead when it was right for them to do so, and make others feel safe in the process.

These were solid foundations. Powerful sentiments. They became our new cultural imperatives.

Framed around these Pillars, the team defined six key principles with associated behaviours. Of course, these will be different for every team. Ours were:

Principle	Behaviour
Trust	I will be trustworthy.
Peer accountability	I will ensure the best of me helps to achieve the best of you.
Self-leadership	I will take ownership as though it all comes down to me.
Openness	I will listen, communicate, and learn without prejudice.
Crucial conversations	I will speak up at the right time, with the right people, in the right way.
Belief	I am committed to our vision, and believe my purpose aligns with it.

The internal marketing team were engaged. Graphic design wheels started turning. Emails launched our new position. Culture Commitments were distributed. Posters were hung. But much more importantly, people bought in.

The theory had been laid. We now needed to behave.

Culture theme park

The bar had been set. Clarity was given. Expectations were managed.

To change culture, people need actionable first steps. We needed to enlarge their capacity and provide new resources to facilitate change. We also had to allow for slips, trips, breaches, and mistakes. People must be afforded grace for change. There is nothing more disempowering than being set an unrealistic objective with no tolerance for learning.

We reflected on the Disney adventure rides. There were at least two options: rollercoasters and merry-go-rounds.

The former was full of difficulties. It was unpredictable. There were slow climbs and fast descents, sharp corners with loud screams, high adrenalin punctuated with fear.

The latter just went around and around. Whether slow or fast, you never travelled anywhere. It didn't have a destination or endpoint. Most likely, it just made you dizzy, nauseous, and frustrated.

We had a choice. What ride did we want to go on?

ONEteam™ was always a choice for adventure. Not reckless abandon, but calculated risks that included the thrill of the unknown. Nobody wanted to go around in circles. We agreed that our ride would have some setbacks, disappointments, frightening moments, and anxious stages. But it also promised progress and excitement.

We boarded the rollercoaster!

We managed our expectations accordingly. We gave ourselves permission to fail and reset. We weren't going to play it safe and fall short. Our new Culture Commitment had to be pursued.

The ancient proverb rang true. *If we wanted the strength of the ox in the field, we had to accept some poop in the stable.* In simple terms, we agreed to take the downside with the upside.

All the benefits of a brave new world were going to have some risks to manage. We conceded we wouldn't get it right every time. Practice would make perfect. Some toes would even get stepped on as we learned the rhythm of a new cultural dance.

The concept of 'J' curves resonated with us. We were prepared to travel downwards a little, to catapult upwards. We believed in the slingshot effect – move backwards slightly to go forwards with confidence. Every skyscraper of steel and glass went downwards first to establish concrete foundations.

Resetting culture was clearly no different. We accepted our path.

Opt in

Every team member was invited on the culture journey. In the same way that 7/50/100 was never imposed, the Culture Commitment was put forward in the form of an offer.

We avoided assumptions. Nobody was deemed committed to our new Culture Pillars and Principles unless they said so. The default position was *out*, until they opted *in*. Every colleague was asked to make an informed decision: full disclosure, free choice, individual consent.

Why? Because *teams* create great culture – not leaders. We needed everyone.

To avoid any doubt, we sought written confirmation of every team members' commitment – a signed contract. A statement of intention that provided for absolute clarity and accountability.

Through the process, one or two self-ejected. As I say, they released themselves to pursue a new adventure. However, to my surprise and delight, we had most commit to the new way of doing things.

They let go of the past... and chose the winding path forwards and upwards, despite the ardour of the climb that awaited. These brave souls become the inaugural composition of ONEteam".

John's story

ONEteam™ provided a much-needed shift in staff culture and colleague accountability. We were overdue and needed it.

The removal of titles and hierarchy instantly created a unified, even playing field for me to explore and familiarise myself with. The new culture allowed me to express my views and ideas freely, knowing that my voice would be heard. New opportunities were laid out before me, giving me the ability to lead and take ownership of the projects that I could contribute best to.

Our new workplace culture was enhanced by the understanding that 'ranking' was no longer a prerequisite for leadership. My ideas and queries would be met with a consistent collaborative review and given equal opportunity for action. This allowed me, and those Colleagues around me, to have our thinking heard, feel appreciated, and really contribute as a valued member of the team.

Previously, I worked hard on project after project, contributing my best, only to watch my managers happily receive all of the public recognition, without even raising an eye in my direction. I would hardly call that fair or equitable. ONEteam™ allowed me to take ownership of my own projects, receive recognition where it was due, and truly rise and fall on my own merit. This became a breath of fresh air.

Stay fresh

All that awaited now was the application. The mouth of *reality* was wide open and ready to bite. We had to live the standard for it to become the culture.

Our Pillars and Principles were woven into the fabric of our new staff inductions, training programs, and performance reviews. We became daily opportunists – reinforcing the right behaviours whenever we could. Constantly pointing to our two Pillars. Acknowledging our culture champions. Even re-cutting performance bonuses to reflect cultural alignment, above all else.

We never wanted the Culture Commitment to live in the drawer. We wanted it written on our hearts. Forefront in our minds. Badged on our uniforms. Emblazoned on the walls of our workplace.

Structured activities protected against vision leak. We actively prevented our culture from waning. We formed a new habit of careful observation. We asked targeted questions (individually and collectively). We gathered intentional feedback. We continuously set direction and posted outcomes around behaviour standards.

Cultural stocktakes prompted a reflective personal inventory of values, beliefs, attributes, and behaviours. We were avoiding accidents at all costs, living our culture on purpose. Consistency became king – and queen.

We didn't want the conversation to stop. When it eventually did, someone would inevitably start it again. We kept the pump primed, the bear poked, and the engine running.

Make it stick

Unfortunately, despite all efforts, culture can be like Teflon. Sometimes nothing sticks!

Words, words, words… You can do it all: surveys, workshops, posters, inspirational stories, contracts, role playing, group exercises, testimonials, vision-casting, core values, and achievement awards. Time passes. People get busy. The message dilutes. Commitments are forgotten. And culture slips. I'm sure you have experienced the same.

There are no surprises here. Size, speed, and scale are the enemy of excellence. If non-vigilant, culture will suffer a recurring injury. Ours did a few times in the first year… and the second year… and each one after that. If you have experienced similar false starts, then we are all in good company.

We learned we could never rest on our laurels. Persistence was the only strategy to make culture stick – repetition!

Some got it quickly. Others struggled. The strong carried the weak at times when we needed everyone to move more quickly. Eventually, the person with the most energy was going to win! I had to be that guy.

Anyone can 'keep it together' for a day... or at least a moment. But how do you make these cultural imperatives the new normal? It needed to become a team habit, a perpetual engine. Change had to be sustained. It couldn't be 'set-and-forget'.

We found we had to keep it personal!

Our cultural attributes became the daily glue of workplace framework. We relied on intentional action from leadership; emphasis on both the written and spoken word; daily accountability with positive and negative consequences; rewards and acknowledgement at every opportunity. Without exception, the cultural goals must be worked into the rhythm of everything you do. You must fight for your culture at all costs!

So, this is what we did. We established our *unwritten* ground rules. Culture stuck. The vision and behaviour of ONEteam™ were aligned. We could finally play the game now. But to win, we needed practice within the structure. Lots of it!

Transferable Principles

23 Culture eats *strategy* for breakfast, *vision* for lunch, and *structure* for dinner.

24 *Teams* create culture, not just leaders.

25 Trust is earned when *actions* meet *words*.

26 Most leaders *assume* their culture is *better* than it really is.

27 If you are not intentionally building a *specific* culture, then you are unintentionally building an *alternative* one.

28 To change culture, people need *actionable* first steps.

29 Culture must become a *commitment*. It's not *set-and-forget*. It's a decision that must be refreshed daily.

6. WORK FLOW

The debate

There is fierce debate within popular culture as to the quintessential component of effective business success.

First there are the **visionaries**!

This group declares that vision is the indispensable quality of leadership. Without setting direction, you lose. You stumble before you even begin. We must cast a bright light for the masses to follow. View the end from the beginning. The notion that anyone can steer a ship is believable, but it takes a leader to chart a course. As Helen Keller profoundly quoted, "the only thing worse than being born blind, would be to have sight without vision."

Then there are the **culture hipsters**.

Remember, culture eats strategy for breakfast. The way things get done trumps the ideology and aspiration of the hopeful, would-be corporate orators. Traditions, feelings, and behaviours matter most. Read the mood of the room correctly, and you are sure to win.

But let's not forget the **pragmatists**.

They are the implementers. People who get stuff done. Those who believe that visionary talk can be cheap; culture is vague; but the real power lies in execution. Ultimately, everything relies on action.

It's the spirit of Nike-ism. *Just Do It.* You need a grand idea, exceeded only by the sensible tactics and strategy necessary to carry it out. Sean Covey teaches in his bestselling book *The 4 Disciplines of Execution* to: prioritise the wildly important; act on lead measures; keep a compelling scorecard; and create a cadence of accountability. His followers can't be persuaded otherwise.

So, who is right? Visionaries, culture hipsters or pragmatists?

I find there is little value in arguing the semantics. I can't artificially separate the benefits. I learned all three must integrate for sustainable success.

As discussed in previous chapters, vision and culture are crucially important. But now I could not afford to miss the execution piece.

The mechanics of work flow matter. All the management theory and re-tooling of a leadership model amounts to little, unless it can be channelled into decisive and effective action. The identity of ONEteam˜ had to be expressed in practical format: tangible, repeatable, and predictable steps. We needed a fresh infusion of not-so-common, *common sense.*

In simple terms, our *thinking* and *feeling* had to convert to *doing.*

The mechanics

Creativity is not enough. Success relies on that idea being actioned. A script eventually needs to be orated. A strategy is nothing until it's implemented.

7/50/100 was our destination. ONEteam˜ was the vehicle to get there. Our purpose, *to be significant,* was the fuel in the tank. Our Culture Commitment defined how we would behave on the road trip.

But we needed a new engine!

The mechanics of our machine had to be re-engineered. We re-bored a few cylinders. Swapped some of the factory-installed options for custom modifications. Imported select new technology.

Our vehicle was getting an upgrade. We installed an on-board computer that synchronised all the moving parts of our high-performance machine. We wanted the precision of a fine timepiece, with the attitude of a Mack Truck.

We searched for effective enablers to convert the theory of this workplace revolution into practice. We identified effective daily steps that could slingshot us toward the goal, with surety of ultimate success. This became our ONEteam™ work flow (see Figure 6.1)!

Figure 6.1: ONEteam™ work flow

MPV_1SV_2

Strategic Target

Priority Goals

Strategies

Balanced Scorecard Indicators

Team Work Plans

Projects and Taskforces

Planning to plan

Many believe strategic planning to be a dark art – practised only by those tethered to the roots of ancient practice; or those with a manipulative agenda. The less sinister and simpler view is that it just doesn't work – that strategic planning is only undertaken to make the non-science of astrology look more credible.

Archive storerooms of corporate headquarters swell with outdated strategic documents… obsolete thinking, memorials to ideas that have expired, and actions that were never taken. The bottom of too many filing cabinets are overflowing with dormant genius strategy that people forget to build work flow around.

We didn't just need a plan! More than this, we needed to action our plan.

As outlined in Chapter 1, we followed a detailed process to unearth, refine, and assert our key identity statements.

MPV₁SV₂: Mission, Purpose, Vision, Strategy, Values.

We knew who we were. Or at least, who we wanted to become.

We understood why we existed.

We had clarity over where we were going, when we wanted to get there, and what we believed in.

We just didn't know yet *how* to make all this happen.

The big picture

Strategy is birthed by soul-searching and hard work – no shortcuts. You shouldn't skimp on the planning phase.

Identity begets mission. And a strategic theme precedes actionable goals.

Multiple whiteboard sessions, brainstorming exercises, rigorous debate, and round table discussions continued to clarify our big picture. We zoned in on our version of Jim Collins' big, hairy, audacious goal – the one wildly important thing, our core.

In the spirit of courageous exploits, all visioneering sessions were freed from over-rational thinking. You can't be too sensible. Welcome a little bit of crazy to the beginning of the meeting. Better to dream the impossibilities first, before you consider the restraints of budget, time, and individual capabilities. Of course, there is a place for these considerations to follow. Just don't limit your thinking in the first instance.

If you don't let your imagination run wild at the beginning, it will never catch up. Sensible thoughts starve creativity. Fill the room with oxygen at the beginning, and breathe it all in.

What would you dare to dream if you were guaranteed you couldn't fail?

That's a profound question. *Read it again.*

What would you dare to dream if you were guaranteed you couldn't fail?

Chase the biggest picture you can capture.

An inspiring, overarching theme must frame each strategic season. In our case, it was 7/50/100! One hundred flagship practices generating $50 million located in 7 states and territories of Australia.

Our strategic plans stand for approximately three years. After this, it's time to recapture a new view of the emerging future. To dream again. Project further beyond the horizon. Re-cast with fresh passion.

The journey of a thousand miles begins with one step.

Less is best

So much has been written about goals: *setting* them, *measuring* them, *reaching* them, *exceeding* them.

Goals are more complicated than most realise. This, at least in part, explains why so many people give up on them. Other reasons are that some are afraid of failure; afraid of success; undisciplined; incompetent; disorganised; lack accountability; don't know their *why*; or simply are too lazy!

It's not that goal-setting doesn't work – we don't work *goals!*

Achieving goals combines both art and science. More is not better. Less is best.

The word *priority* is deceptive. Derived from the Medieval Latin form *prioritatem*, it has only a singular iteration – no plural. Priority was never intended to infer more than one. In the western world, we have distorted its meaning by making it bigger than it was ever intended to be. We want multiple. We think bigger is better. We believe more is *more*. Just like with our approach to the traditional Italian pizza – we take a simple food and add three times the topping to *improve* it. The problem is, we don't make it better!

In our goal-setting, we end up with multiple priorities. It's an oxymoron. You can't have more than one priority. It creates competing attention, split focus, fragmented emphasis, and distracted effort.

The United Nations has 20 Priority Goals. 20!

The World Health Organization has 8 Leadership Priorities.

The Australian Institute of Company Directors has 6 reform priorities in their 2017 scorecard for the Governance of the Nation.

I also used to have 10 to 12 personal goals every year. You probably do too.

It's too many! We need less, if we want to be effective.

Priority Goals

I afforded ONEteam™ only four Priority Goals! It's not one, but it was better than 12.

Each goal had to align and build the story of our Strategic Theme. A cascading effort – four milestones toward a final achievement.

The Priority Goals for Back In Motion during our season of 7/50/100 are summarised in Figure 6.2. It was about developing individual and collective team capabilities to then build scalable business systems. It then became about sourcing funding and investments to pay for new people and better infrastructure, so that we could explosively grow the footprint.

Figure 6.2: The Priority Goals of 7/50/100

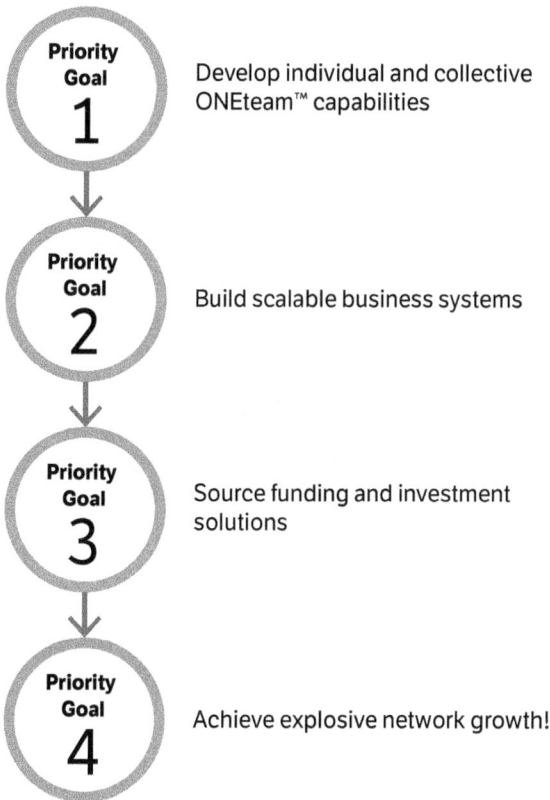

Priority Goal 1	Develop individual and collective ONEteam™ capabilities
Priority Goal 2	Build scalable business systems
Priority Goal 3	Source funding and investment solutions
Priority Goal 4	Achieve explosive network growth!

The goals told a sensible narrative. Achieving one made it more likely we would succeed with the next. They built on each other.

In the true sense of the word, the one and only priority was the final goal. We had to achieve explosive network growth. However, we all realised that just saying it was so, would not make it happen. We needed to do the preparatory work first.

We had to invest internally in ourselves. We then needed to engineer systems that would support new growth. We also had to build the confidence in others around us to provide the necessary capital to invest. The network footprint could only be sustained if the initial three goals were achieved first.

We were willing to go backwards, and sideways, to go forwards. We dug downward first. Laid the proper foundations before we put up the steel and glass. There was method in our madness. *Outside-in downside-up*!

Goals without deadlines are just suggestions. We wanted mandates. We assigned a measurable outcome and timeframe to each milestone – with no guessing, no grey areas, no dodging. We had our priority to pursue.

Key Strategic Objectives

The next stage in our work flow was to convert the thinking of our Priority Goals into more articulate Strategic Objectives.

How do you eat an elephant? *One bite at a time.*

We underpinned every Priority Goal with a series of statements that boldly declared *how* we would achieve them. Because more is not better, we restricted our Strategic Objectives to only a handful for each goal – the big rocks, the key deliverables we believed would be responsible for the greatest impact.

Our plan was starting to take shape (see Figure 6.3).

Figure 6.3: Back In Motion 7/50/100 Strategic Plan

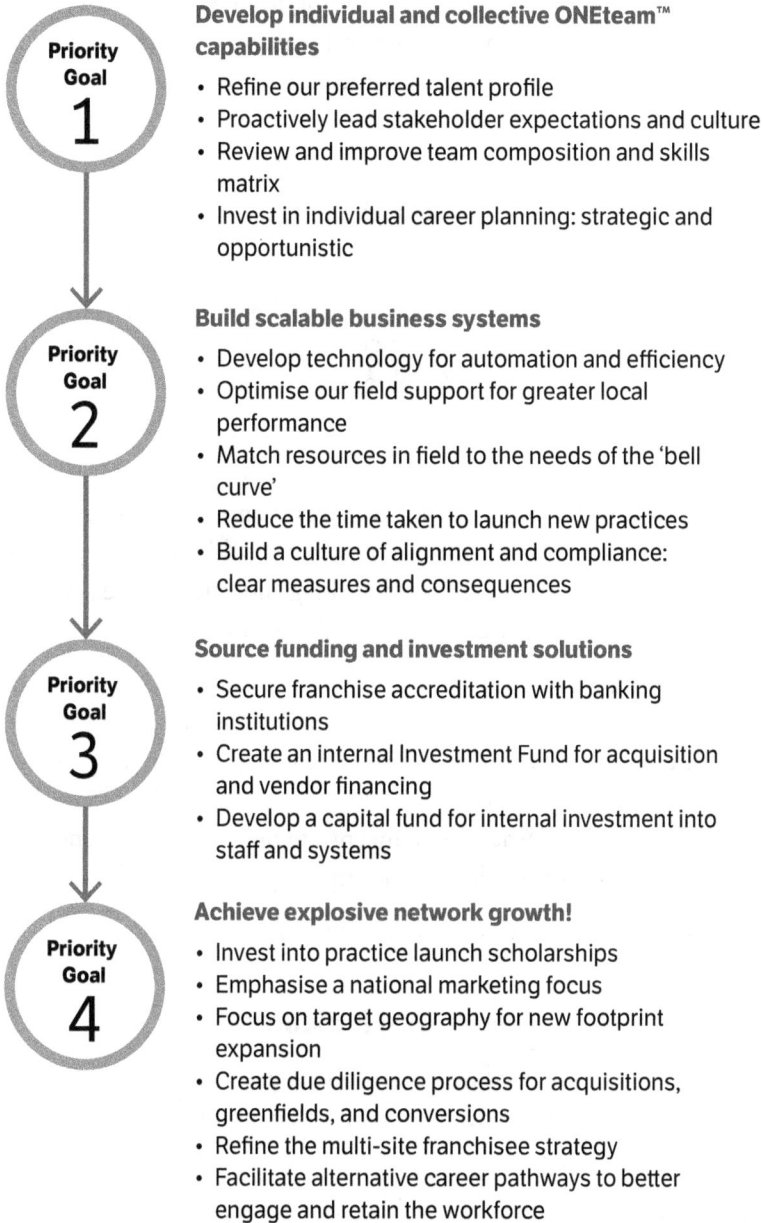

Priority Goal 1

Develop individual and collective ONEteam™ capabilities

- Refine our preferred talent profile
- Proactively lead stakeholder expectations and culture
- Review and improve team composition and skills matrix
- Invest in individual career planning: strategic and opportunistic

Priority Goal 2

Build scalable business systems

- Develop technology for automation and efficiency
- Optimise our field support for greater local performance
- Match resources in field to the needs of the 'bell curve'
- Reduce the time taken to launch new practices
- Build a culture of alignment and compliance: clear measures and consequences

Priority Goal 3

Source funding and investment solutions

- Secure franchise accreditation with banking institutions
- Create an internal Investment Fund for acquisition and vendor financing
- Develop a capital fund for internal investment into staff and systems

Priority Goal 4

Achieve explosive network growth!

- Invest into practice launch scholarships
- Emphasise a national marketing focus
- Focus on target geography for new footprint expansion
- Create due diligence process for acquisitions, greenfields, and conversions
- Refine the multi-site franchisee strategy
- Facilitate alternative career pathways to better engage and retain the workforce

A balanced life

When the stakes are high in a nail-biting football final, all eyes are on the scoreboard. As the seconds count down, the tension builds. You can tell a lot about what is happening on the field by just looking at the score.

All sports keep score in some way or another. And ONEteam™ is a team sport. With goals and strategies in place, we needed our own scoreboard.

Organisations all over the world have introduced infographics, dashboards, and scorecards to create a culture of peer accountability and to celebrate achievement. We value what we measure, and what we measure can be managed.

As a long-time advocate for the Balanced Scorecard, it was time to take the best of Kaplan and Norton's work, and modify to suit. We needed to synthesise the right metrics that would reveal the greatest gains toward our end – with lead and lag indicators – a dashboard with all the right measures to guide and affirm us.

At times, running an organisation our size feels like sitting in the cockpit of a 747... more dials, knobs, levers, buttons, and switches than one brain can assimilate. Inputs and outputs. Digital displays. Graphs and readings. Elevations, altitude, speed, landing gear, fuel, and cabin pressure. What do I concentrate on? Surely, each one can't be as important as the other! Or are they?

Frustratingly, it depends on the circumstances.

Dashboard indicators

The traditional Balanced Scorecard pivots itself on achieving a central strategy. It measures progress via four quadrants in order of cause and effect (see Figure 6.4).

The underlying premise of the Balanced Scorecard is that financial metrics are insufficient indicators of team performance and the value being created (or destroyed) in our business.

Investment into the first three quadrants, in the prescribed order, will inevitably deliver the desired financial outcomes. Concentrate on first things first. Make people, systems, and then customers your focus, and the dollars will follow.

Figure 6.4: Kaplan and Norton's Traditional Balanced Scorecard

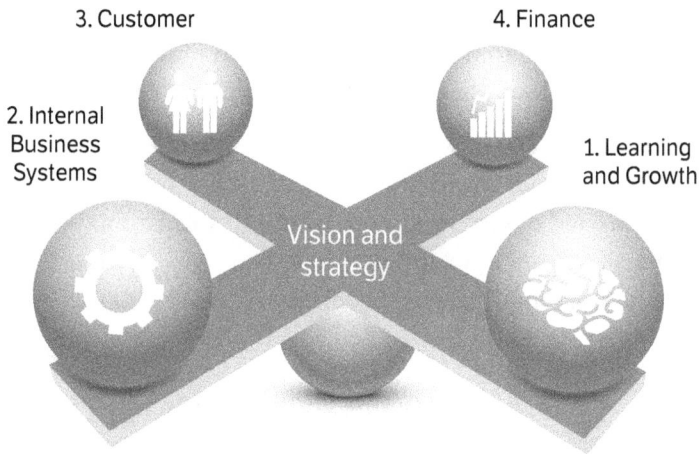

Keeping it simple, we modelled our four quadrants as the four Ps: People, Processes, Patients, and Pennies (see Figure 6.5 overleaf).

We learned that whatever format your scorecard takes on, it must have some consistent attributes.

They all should be:

- **Strategic in nature** – The scorecard must measure what is important to you. Sometimes we end up measuring numbers because they are obvious and easy – but might not be relevant. We had to pin each deliverable to a Priority Goal, or it was dumped.

- **Mutually negotiated** – All Colleagues contributed to the design of the measures. Not just the types, but also the quantum of each target. It's no use imposing a threshold that others don't buy into. It's better to have the argy-bargy at the front end of the process than after the deadline has passed. Invite disagreement. Facilitate peer competitiveness. Allow all boats to rise on the same tide.

- **Aligned** – Cause and effect should link measures. The relationship between activity and outcomes must be certain. Distinction should be created between lead indicators (which predict performance) and lag indicators (which give evidence of actual results).

- **Objective** – A scorecard must be interpretable by all team members and observers without need for explanation. The numbers must be firm and incontestable – no subjective measures, no motherhood statements, no wriggle room!

Figure 6.5: 7/50/100 Modified Scorecard

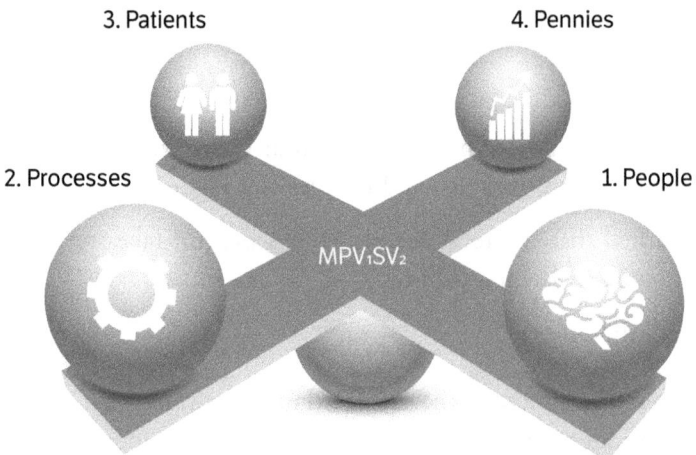

- **Clearly documented** – If it's not written down, it didn't happen. The scorecard can't be imagined, only spoken of, or infrequently referred to. It needs to be documented in full and published regularly. It's the basis of all conversations that pertain to strategy and performance. In our case, it was a live electronic screen in the bullpen. Visible to all – a constant reminder.

- **Positively reinforced** – Whatever you focus on, you get more of. All awards, bonuses, platitudes, gratitude, and celebrations should be directly linked to positive performance on the scorecard. If you fail to reinforce the right behaviour, you are powerless to change the wrong behaviour.

Accelerators and oil lights

It dawned on me that the dashboard of my Harley Davidson has two types of indicators: an accelerator and an oil light. One tells me how fast I'm going. The other warns me of impending problems. One positive, one negative – it is a balanced scorecard for riding safely.

I wanted the same for ONEteam™. Accelerators on our scorecard were to become the stretch targets that promoted performance in our strategic direction. They would measure our speed getting there.

We had many metrics to measure, including:

- quality and frequency of franchise conversions
- number of new sites
- how many months to launch a practice
- practice sales and profitability
- workforce retention
- processing days for reporting compliance activities.

We wanted pace in each of these metrics. Speed was good, as long as the dashboard didn't show any oil lights as we accelerated.

The oil lights were those measures on our scorecard that cautioned us against underperformance, failure in key areas that would limit achievement of our strategic objectives. For instance:

- patient complaints

- staff resignations

- quality control issues in process activities

- debt ratios

- escalating fixed costs

- cultural breaches.

Accelerators set uppermost limits to reach for. Oil lights set lowermost limits we would tolerate before causing alarm.

If the dashboard didn't show any red oil lights, then the unspoken message was to keep accelerating at full throttle toward all the aspirational targets ahead. Any time a warning appeared, however, we slowed down, took the corner safely, shored up the quality of our performance, and made sure we didn't blow the engine. Only when the oil lights disappeared would we accelerate again.

Stunt driving is not without its risks. We value precision and high performance over the brashness of a bang-up derby.

Budget negotiations

Eventually, in all these things, the money does matter.

Vision, priority goals, strategic objectives, and measurable scorecards eventually rely on resourcing.

The most limited resources at our disposal are time, people, and money. Of these, time is unredeemable. It's therefore the most precious. People and relationships are crucial, but we rely on time to show value to others.

When budgets are negotiated, we think it's only about the money. This is wrong. What about time and people?

Our budgeting exercises sought to estimate the financial cost of investing into new strategies, but also the temporal and human costs.

How long will it take?

Who will do it?

How much money is required?

What opportunities are we saying 'no' to, so we can say 'yes' to others?

The old school approach of departments holding onto last year's budget allocation as a right or entitlement was killed.

We are one team, remember: ONEteam™. With no silos, no barricades, no turf wars, no territorialism. What's mine is yours. Including my provision from last year's budget. If it is better distributed to a different Function within the business to achieve their Mandate, then we all win!

Our team had to learn a new approach to budget negotiations. Our workplace revolution released all time, people, and financial resources of the organisation to those who would most benefit from them. It was a clean start on a zero cost basis. We built our new budget from the ground up, with our vision as the guide.

Work Plans

With all that said, the talking had to give way to doing.

Blueprints were written. Plans were drawn. Intention was clear. Measures were agreed. Money was distributed.

Champions and Advocates gathered their Function Colleagues together in small huddles. It was time for elbow grease. Shoulders leaned against the plough. Sweat beaded on brows. Each Function constructed their own Work Plan: a self-directed document that articulated all the tasks and actions they would take. It was the outline of their best contribution to ONEteam™.

Work Plans are crucial outlines. They demonstrate the substance of the real work being done on a day-by-day basis – the who's who of the what's what. Not a conceptual plan, but a very tactical, specific, and detailed description of exactly what must happen, by whom, and when.

Dates matter. Budget is critical. The owner of each task is held to account – as per the Culture Commitment. Neglect is not an option. The Work Plan becomes our judge and jury with regards to performance assessment.

The Strategy and Innovation Executive Pod is responsible for carefully choreographing the Work Plans of each Function. They ensure the hand fits the glove.

Work Plans became the centrepiece for weekly Function meetings (if not daily). Activity was only deemed accomplishment if it progressed the Work Plan.

The Work Plans are designed as living documents that bend and flex to unplanned obstacles, interrelated activities of other Functions, and new directives of ONEteam™. If I was ever in doubt how well a Function was performing – I'd look at their Work Plan.

Projects and Taskforces

One of the great prizes of this leadership revolution was the collaboration evident across old team boundaries. We started to enjoy true cross-functional input. Working together, rather than just working in the same room – with alignment and inter-connectedness.

No *one* is as smart as *all* of us. True teamwork became the highest order of achievement in our progressive workplace model. It had no boundaries.

We could not afford paygrade to separate Colleagues. Technical Function was not a distinction to isolate or fragment. Experience and tenure were irrelevant. Qualifications and levels of responsibility weren't to discriminate.

We were all on the same side and wanted the same thing. The big picture mattered. We had four Priority goals that depended on all of us working together.

When any Work Plans were reviewed, it was obvious to everyone that we would all suffer if any Colleague felt isolated.

Marketing and Communications relied on input from Business Intelligence and Technology to launch new websites and capitalise on the social media juggernaut.

The Finance, Risk, and Administration Function needed field context and interpretative insights from Practice Support and Performance to explain what the monthly finance reports were showing.

The Network Development Function relied heavily on People and Systems to facilitate the pipeline of franchisee enquiry.

We all needed each other. This gave rise to the notion of Projects and Taskforces.

A Project became any special-purpose activity that drew Colleagues from multiple Functions to deliver on specific outcomes in a finite timeframe.

In contrast, a Taskforce differed in that it could also involve other con-tributors from outside ONEteam™. These could include franchisees, suppliers, industry advisors, clients, patients, or other stakeholders from our value-chain.

Any Colleague who was suitably experienced could become a Project or Taskforce Lead.

Open book

Our work style became something that reflected the idealistic intentions of ONEteam™.

We became one! With no hidden agenda, no surprises, no politics, no unnecessary hierarchy. Elitism was dead – along with sensitive documents, confidential memos, and closed-door meetings.

We strived for trust and transparency – something we liked to call *trustparency*. Nobody was expected to work on a need-to-know basis. We preferred the *want-to-know* paradigm. If you were interested, then we were willing.

Life in ONEteam™ became an open book.

Strategy documents were posted online. Detailed financial statements were made available to all. Full budget allocations were disclosed. Even people's payroll arrangements were published in an open-source format to show that all the sacred cows had been euthanised.

Transparency was a key culture component. If we expected the hands to work hard, we had to ensure the hearts were aligned.

Malcolm's story

I couldn't understand why Jason or the Board would be willing to disclose all of the financials of the business to the team. I came from a conservative mindset, where these details were best kept confidential from most people. It seemed like we were asking for trouble. Most people probably wouldn't understand them anyway.

I was worried some people might use the data against us. Maybe to negotiate a personal advantage at salary review time, or just be careless in how they talked with others outside the business.

Soon after, I realised I was probably being too cautious. Even though I work in finance, I enjoyed and benefited from getting copies of the marketing plans and HR reports. So, what did it matter if everyone knew our profit statements and balance sheets? Maybe it will help inform better decision making. If nothing else, we couldn't be accused of hiding anything.

This was just one of the many changes we underwent as we re-thought our workflow and habits in the office.

The magic

In the end, any Strategic Target will only be achieved because Projects, Taskforces, and Work Plan activities are undertaken every day by real people in concert with each other. There's no mystery, no magic – just hard and smart work. Attributes I'm sure you are familiar with.

The numbers, project templates, and ONEteam™ work flow are the mechanical tools in the hands of the real heroes: our Colleagues. People matter. This wouldn't be a revolution if it didn't involve the blood, sweat, and tears of mortals. People are always the heart and soul of any organisation.

With fresh structure, a Culture Commitment, new management theory, and a re-tooled work flow, we still needed to care for our people differently. If we didn't get this right, ONEteam™ would all be for nothing.

Transferable Principles

30 The mechanics of work flow matter. At some point the *thinking* must convert to *doing*.

31 *Less* is best. The fewer priorities, the more likely you will *retain focus* and *achieve* them.

32 Workplace leadership is a *team sport*, so it needs a *scoreboard* – lead and lag measures.

33 Vision must be resourced – so plan and budget for *people*, *time*, and *money*!

34 Embrace *trust* parency. Nurture a *want-to-know* culture rather than keeping people on a *need-to-know* basis.

7. PEOPLE

People are the reason

People matter. They are the reason we do anything. At least, this should always be true.

The purpose drives our *why*. The mission infers our *what*. The vision sets our *where*. The strategy defines our *how*. But people are the glue that holds all this together. They are the heart of the organisation – our collective soul.

People define our culture. Our culture sets the tone of the experience of every stakeholder – both within and outside the team.

Great people are the prize of effective leadership. They are the heroes of every workplace story. They are both the *means* and the *end*.

Do well

There are fewer things I want more than to see my people thrive.

I want them to experience personal success and fulfilment – to reach dizzy heights. To achieve beyond their dreams, exceed expectations, go to unimaginable places.

I want them to feel the thrill of professional excellence, expert craftsmanship, and deft skill, with insightful judgement. I want them to stand head and shoulders above the norm, and be highly esteemed

– the gold standard, beyond reproach. I want them to be wildly successful, the envy of their peers.

My hope for them is to go further, faster; and grow bigger, stronger. I really want them to *do* well.

I expect they do too.

Accordingly, they should be well rewarded for their efforts. Their loyalty and work ethic should yield bountiful return, career progression, financial gain, rich experience, professional development, personal satisfaction, and community impact.

But doing well is only part of the story.

Be well

More than *doing* well, I want our people to *be* well.

We are human *beings*, not human *doings*. We need to be well in body, soul, and spirit. Healthy people are better than smart ones. Self-care is essential. In this fast paced, manic world, *being* well is a precursor to *doing* well.

Our people needed to learn to look after themselves better than before. It was the only way to be at our best. We couldn't lead and empower others unless we learnt how to achieve this for ourselves. Learning to swim was a prerequisite to saving someone else from drowning.

Health, happiness, alignment… these are all high ideals in the workplace – but for many, long forgotten.

Our workplace revolution recognised those who were *un*well. The many who had lost ground to progressive tiredness and confusion… with looming burnout. We saw lots of strained activity and exhausted souls.

It wasn't just mind over matter. Deep rest and recalibration was necessary. Being well became a strategic imperative.

Best contribution

Only well people can offer their best contribution to the team. This became an obvious truth.

Every team member had skills, experience, and passions, and aspirations they wanted to grow into. What a shame that most jobs pigeon hole people into arbitrary confines. We are often asked to be and do certain things that don't feel compatible... a poor fit, square pegs in round holes.

Many spend 80% of their time doing what they are only 20% equipped for – like a reverse Pareto principle. We needed to change this. We wanted the right pegs in the right holes; people doing at least 80% of the work they are built for.

Everyone considered what their best contribution to the team looked like.

What can only I do?

What can I do substantively better than anyone else?

If I wasn't in the team, what would we miss?

We aligned passion and expertise, with genuine organisational need.

Role Profiles

People's best contributions needed to be documented.

Every treasure hunt needs a map. We wanted nothing left to chance.

Old job requirements and static position descriptions were shelved. Clean sheets of paper were produced. Pencils were sharpened.

We drafted new tools: *Role Profiles*. Role Profiles outlined the best contribution each person could be relied upon to advance our team and achieve our mission. Every profile was mutually negotiated and agreed. No two looked the same. They were to remain fluid until a better fit was discovered.

Each profile was posted on the organisational intranet to engender a collective understanding of a Colleague's performance expectations. The magic lay in the sweet spot between technical competencies, natural talents, and individual passions.

The Role Profiles clearly itemised core work descriptions as the essential roles, responsibilities, and contributions of each Colleague. Secondary Work Descriptions captured adjunctive and supportive roles.

Role Profiles became tools for empowerment. They were designed as great enablers. Colleagues were expected to make responsible decisions within clearly identified limits. All delegated authorities were unique to each person and could not be transferred or assumed through proxy.

With privilege comes responsibility. Accountabilities were put in place. These freedoms only work when people are committed to act in the best interests of the organisation.

Objective results were important. Agreed quantitative and qualitative measures were assigned to each responsibility. Regular review of performance and contribution to ONEteam™ ensured progress.

We quickly realised that a new support framework was needed to review Role Profiles in real time.

Lines of support

Traditional models of management pride themselves on their lines of report.

ONEteam™ doesn't. We replaced lines of *report* with lines of *support* (see Figure 7.1). We gathered around our people rather than hovered from above. We developed the art of *selling* and *compelling*, rather than relying on *telling*.

In our new vogue, I freely gave lots of opinions… but very few instructions. If I couldn't compel you on the basis of logic, strategy, risk, and consequences, then my idea might be flawed. The best way we know to support each other is to allow choices on an informed basis.

To be and do well, every Colleague is nominated a support team.

The responsibility of the First Level Support (1S) is predominantly peer welfare. They also provide performance coaching, continuous feedback, and advocacy on matters such as remuneration assessments and workplace disputes. The 1S is consulted in any proposed changes to the Role Profile. They play an integral role in the Colleague's career planning.

Figure 7.1: First, second and third levels of support

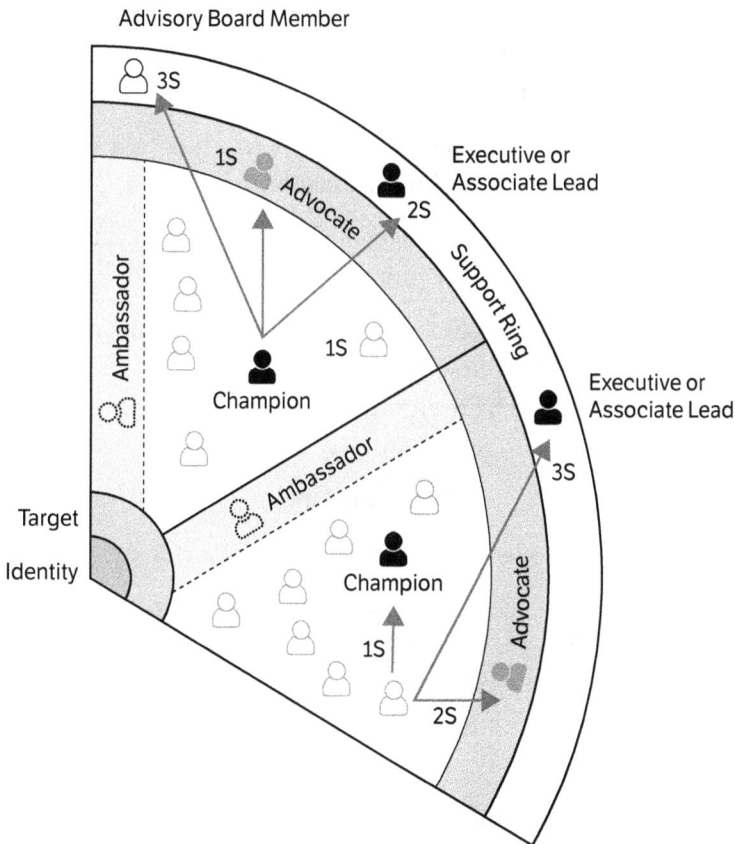

In many cases, the Function Champion is the 1S for their Function Colleagues. The Advocate is the 1S for the Function Champion. The Executive Lead is the 1S for the Support Ring Colleagues. And the Chair of the Advisory Board is the 1S for the Executive Lead. This may vary based on the Colleague's preference.

Every Colleague is further supported by another.

The Second Level Support (2S) is critical in those instances where the role of 1S is inadequate, unavailable, or the relationship has broken down. The 2S also primarily drives cross-Function collaboration through the benefit of being one step removed. Arms-length objectivity is highly valued.

In many cases the Advocate is the 2S for the Function Colleagues. The Executive Lead is the 2S for the Function Champions.

Every Colleague has the added benefit of referring to a Colleague from the Support Ring for direct assistance.

This Third Level Support (3S) is made up of the Executive Lead, Associate Lead(s) and Colleagues of the Advisory Board.

Without support, leadership fails. People don't care how much you know, until they know how much you care. A servant heart underscores the power of ONEteam™. All for one, and one for all.

Going full circle

In the planetary model of ONEteam™, we repel hierarchy.

We don't work *for* each other, but *with* each other. We serve the *mission* rather than the boss. Lines of communication and support have replaced uni-directional lines of report. Our spherical model has no up or down. It's egalitarian. We promote fairness, not sameness; equity, not equality.

People want different things from their workplace. While united by the same cause, they value benefits in unique ways. ONEteam™ recognises individuality in the context of team. Each person is on their own journey – a personal adventure. Their odyssey drives different choices and preferences within their career path.

Leaders within the workplace must help keep a light to their path.

We introduced Full Circle Development Plans (FCDPs) to replace historical career goals. FCDPs are individual documents, uniquely tailored. They are enablers of professional growth, career planning, and talent optimisation. They are designed to encourage both formal and informal occasions of peer review, personal goal-setting, ongoing professional education, and intentional mentoring.

Carefully considered time horizons matter. 90-day objectives informed the short term. 12-month goals outlined the medium term. Priorities for the next three years identified the long-term perspective. Life after three years could be considered too, but generally as part of aspirational conversation rather than a formal roadmap.

People could initiate review of their FCDP as often as it benefited them. Otherwise, it happened at least twice yearly. The 1S was the chief facilitator for this reflection exercise and exploration of development opportunities for each Colleague.

Live, in person

Career planning hinges on meaningful performance review.

Typically, performance reviews are done badly. They are infrequent, and thus irrelevant. They are subjective, and thus lack measurable rigour. They are either overly positive or unfairly critical – because the reviewer lacks empathy and expertise to deliver a balanced report.

Colleagues often see reviews as a thinly veiled and ineffective process to determine pay increases. They become a bonus review more than performance review. If so, transparency and honest reflection on self-performance is too risky.

The net result: most performance reviews are unhelpful. Or maybe worse, even counter-productive.

Knowing all this, we had to do things differently. The traditional approach didn't work. At best, performance reviews offered only one person's opinion. But we were a team… ONEteam˝. We wanted a team review – not the boss's review.

It had to be regular, objective, well-rounded, constructive, and not linked directly to remuneration. We needed candour, but not at the risk of safety. We needed to encourage one another, but without flattery.

In one of our most radical initiatives in this workplace revolution, we introduced live Round Table performance reviews. One hot seat. Six peers. Forty-five minutes. In an unprecedented human social experiment, every Colleague was invited to participate in their own live review.

The 1S chaired the review, and the composition of the room was made up of a cross-section of ONEteam˝ – a true 360 degrees.

The narrative of each live review was balanced. It included reflections on core work description, delegated responsibilities, key accountabilities, performance strengths and opportunities, and cultural behaviour. Focus was given to enhancing key relationships and contribution to MPV_1SV_2.

The brave went first. We stumbled a bit. Practice made perfect. Confidence slowly grew.

I was not exempt from any of these experiences. I had my turn in the middle of the room, like everyone else.

Team members needed to develop the art of meaningful feedback, respectful candour, solutions-focused suggestions, and succinct communication. Assertions had to be accompanied by real examples.

Trust was tested. We had to take care of the heart, as well as satisfy the mind. Sensitivities were heeded, and emotional intelligence fostered.

With a mix of personal responses, the overwhelming feedback after the first round was positive. It was scary, unconventional, and unpredictable – yes! But no different from any thrill ride at the theme park.

And we were all in the same boat. We were being authentic. We made ourselves vulnerable. No one was above the mission. We were being truly accountable to each other.

The good news is, live feedback worked. It was here to stay. This became part of our new team fabric.

Colin's story

A definite positive of ONEteam™, in my view, was the introduction of Round Table live performance reviews for all Colleagues. This format provided team members real-time feedback on their performance from various Colleagues within the organisation. The beauty of this approach was that feedback was not solely given by one person, traditionally the direct line manager. The Colleague benefited from feedback right across their working sphere, including via people in different Functions who probably have a unique perspective or different working relationship with them.

For live performance reviews to work, however, they firstly rely on people who are providing the feedback to feel safe enough to give open and honest observations. Secondly, it requires the person receiving the feedback to be open-minded, relaxed, and not take the inbound critique personally.

In my first round of live performance reviews, I don't think we had the maturity to carry it off. Not everyone felt safe enough to be open and honest in their feedback. What resulted was a series of predominantly overly positive affirmation sessions that unearthed very little constructive criticism for the Colleague to take away and work on. There were a small minority who were more authentic and balanced in their appraisals, but these were mostly the more experienced leaders and recently de-titled managers of our old model. Nonetheless, it was obvious to everyone that the benefits of these sessions were far greater than the more traditional one-on-one sessions.

We got much better at live reviews with practice. In the second round, six months later, more people contributed with honesty and safety.

I am a big fan of the Full Circle Development Plans, although I accept they are not the easiest sessions to host, contribute to, or be the subject of.

Money matters

At the heart of the social contract in any team is fair reward.

We all invest our lives into causes for different reasons. We also value different benefits. But money lies central to most people's matrix of desire. Money is not evil. The love of it may be. But finance drives the flywheels of society. It's an indispensable part of life.

We were naive if we thought our ONEteam˜ revolution could be silent on the matter. So, we weren't. We talked about the taboo. Money had to become a safe topic in the workplace. We opened the books. All passwords on our financial spreadsheets were deleted – no hidden figures.

Sales, costs, and profits became fully available. Performance against budget on a line-item basis could be assessed by anyone. Regular finance reports were distributed. Full financial visibility was offered.

I was demonstrating, it was no longer *my* money; but *our* money. These were the resources available to achieve our organisational purpose. We had to be great stewards.

As part of this, our financial arrangement with staff had to be fair. Remuneration needed to be reviewed.

We looked for help. We digested market benchmarks, valid research, industry awards, and peer comparatives. We considered years of experience, qualifications, performance, and supply and demand. And of course, affordability.

All these attributes were considered.

We re-set normal: payroll *ground zero*. All Colleagues were assessed against a new framework. With adjustments where necessary, everyone was poised at the right starting line. With money not a dirty word any more, we could move forward.

In the context of ONEteam˜ now, any Colleague could request a remuneration assessment at any time. They just needed a justifiable case.

I didn't sit in judgement. There was no one person with unilateral decision-making power. A peer review panel decided each request.

Our budget had a total salary cap. Step changes in base salaries, or newly approved incentives, had to be afforded within the cap.

This was a self-regulating payroll system. We had to work together… scary, again, but real!

Team members had to grow up very quickly. We had a finite financial envelope in which to move. Idealism was dismantled, and reality bit hard. We couldn't pay disproportionate and unsustainable salaries. If we gave more to some, it meant we would have to give less to others. We relied on alternative strategies to engage and motivate our people.

While money mattered, the mission mattered more. The real prize was being part of a team that wanted to work and achieve together.

Bailey's story

Possibly the most challenging part of the ONEteam™ transition was the overnight accessibility to everyone's salaries. Instantly people started to compare theirs to others. I know I did. It was hard not to.

It would be utopian to think that overnight people suddenly stop caring about stature and salary. We agreed in theory that we needed to see the value of a Colleague in their contribution and not their title – but when salaries were disparate, this was harder for some to accept in reality.

Eventually we came to realise that accountability still required measurement, and that Role Profiles needed to be lived in order to assess the value of any given Colleague. Quality, not quantity, became critical in determining if someone deserved a step change in salary; and even then, with a panel determining the fate of the matter, Colleagues had to sincerely trust who they worked with.

It was a clunky part of the process at first, but we braved it and fought to make it work. We believed in ONEteam™ and knew that in time, we would all learn to adjust. Slowly we did.

Intersections and crossroads

Of all the challenges associated with ONEteam˝, career progression has been one of the most complex.

In our new world of deconstructed hierarchy, some struggled to understand what career progress looks like. It's almost counter-intuitive. The word *promotion* is obsolete. You can't move *up*. Every role is a crucial contributor to the whole. None of us are smarter than all of us. We are inter-dependent.

But nobody wants to stand still. Individuals shouldn't stall. We want to grow – learn, develop, be challenged, expand our skills. Take on more responsibility, and enlarge our capacity. Earn more. Achieve greater things. And why shouldn't we?

The hidden beauty of ONEteam˝ is its infinite flexibility. It's a canvas for the creative to paint their own picture on. Choose your own adventure – pick a path.

Colleagues can keep re-defining their best contribution. Their Role Profiles are fluid. They can lead when they naturally are the right person to do so.

As someone's contribution changes and their measurable impact increases, their reward within the team develops. They represent a strengthening of another Pillar. There's no need for a position to become vacant. We don't fuss with title changes. Remuneration can increase to reflect their contribution. Acknowledgement should be freely given.

Did we build traditional pathways? No! But you shouldn't be surprised by now.

Do intersections of opportunity always appear obvious? No, again. But they readily exist.

Do people get stuck at some crossroads? Sometimes. But the observations and insights of the 1S and 2S become crucial.

It remains the greatest challenge of ONEteam˝, to avoid letting people get lost in space. The model provides freedom to move in any direction. It's agile and responsive. It can adapt quickly when demanded. But this doesn't avoid some Colleagues getting stuck.

There is no substitute for an individual's creative drive that seeks out more opportunity. We can only continue to emphasise the signposts.

Dispute resolution

As you presumably intuit, ONEteam™ is not a perfect model. Back In Motion is not a perfect business. I'm not a perfect leader. Even if I said we were, you wouldn't believe me.

Workplaces are often defined by their vulnerabilities and short-comings. We make mistakes. Not everyone can agree. Perceptions become reality. People get hurt. Truthfully, there is rarely one way to do something. Two people can approach the same matter differently, and both be right. Or both be wrong!

A world that unites people attracts tension. It's universal. It's the price we pay for the power of *team*. If everyone always agreed with me, I wouldn't need them most of the time. Loyal opposition is an attribute of the secure. Respectful disagreement makes for insightful debate. Rigorous conversation, without ego and politics, is a mark of mature Colleagues.

The sign of a great team is not universal agreement or immediate consensus. Debate and disruption is inevitable. Champion teams learn how to navigate their differences, resolve their conflict, and settle their disputes.

ONEteam™ is a vote for boldness. We have opted for candour and forthrightness. We built an anti-fragile system that improves in response to stress and volatility.

Any time a contested difference of opinion arises, we encourage proactivity. No avoidance is allowed. Heads must be pulled from the sand (and anywhere else they shouldn't be!). Colleagues are encouraged to settle issues directly with the person concerned. We promote clear communication, sound argument, mutual respect, and emotional intelligence.

There's no telling tales to the boss – because there isn't one anymore.

If the first attempt fails, then people are encouraged to pause… sleep on it, then re-connect in a day, and attempt another conversation. High stakes and unresolvable matters could involve the respective 1S and 2S parties as required. This fosters objective review and mediation if necessary.

In the rare instances where a conclusion still can't be reached, the matter may be escalated as last resort to a peer review panel. The High Court of ONEteam˚ is the people themselves. All disputes ultimately get judged in context with our mission and Culture Commitment.

Right of appeal

Every fair system or workplace model must provide a right of appeal.

This is true of ONEteam˚. When unsatisfied with a decision, Colleagues are encouraged to strive to fully understand the situation. They need to talk with those who are directly responsible, ask appropriate questions, and explore the concerns.

If required, people can seek objective counsel from their 1S and 2S if still unsatisfied with the decision.

A peer review panel will ultimately be relied upon if any Colleague feels an injustice has occurred.

The holy grail

The common thread throughout this chapter is the value of people. People are our greatest prize – our reason for everything.

People only flourish when placed in safe and constructive environments. Traditional workplaces have traded on fear and pressure. Top-down authority can easily shift to oppression and intimidation – creating an *us* and *them.*

ONEteam™ turns this *outside-in* and *downside-up*. We encourage self-leadership, inclusive culture, empowerment of the individual, and cross-Function collaboration. We strive for a culture of mutual cohesion. None of us wins, unless all of us do.

The holy grail of an effective workplace culture is peer accountability. This is the pot of gold at the end of the rainbow, the mirage in the distance, the oasis in the desert. This is where the *best of me* elicits the *best of you*.

So many strive for it and fall short. It's an illusion to many – an unattainable ideal.

But we can't stop. ONEteam™ relies on it. Our mission demands it.

The glue that binds this model together is the courage to call each other out when we wander off track. It's the humility to accept that people will do the same to you. It's the willingness to take full responsibility. It's the recognition that any behaviour you walk past and accept, creates the culture you deserve.

If you see it, you must own it. None of us can wait for someone else to do it.

Remember the four team members named Everybody, Somebody, Anybody, and Nobody?

> *There was an important job to be done and Everybody was sure that Somebody would do it. Anybody could have done it, but Nobody did it. Somebody got angry about that, because it was Everybody's job. Everybody thought Anybody could do it, but Nobody realised that Everybody wouldn't do it. It ended up that Everybody blamed Somebody when Nobody did what Anybody could have.*

Our people took responsibility. They realised team life had changed, and with that, so must they.

Of course, it's one thing to shift in the heart and mind. We had to change our traditional work format for *best theory* to become *best practice*.

Transferable Principles

35 It's all about the people. They are the collective soul of the workplace. They are both the *means* and the *end* to achieving vision.

36 *Being* well precedes *doing* well.

37 Replace lines of *report* with lines of *support*.

38 Immediate consensus is not the sign of a great team. *Respectful candour* and *rigorous debate* reflect true team maturity.

39 At the heart of the social team contract is *fair reward.*

40 Every fair workplace system must provide a *right of appeal.*

41 *Peer accountability* is the holy grail of team leadership. The *best of me* should elicit the *best of you.*

8. FORMAT

Function and form

Substance over style is essential. And function above form is necessary.

But who said you had to choose?

The best thinking and feeling should be packaged into the right format and structure to achieve optimal impact.

The ONEteam™ model is predicated on the belief that structure serves purpose. But that doesn't mean structure is unimportant. With all the changes in our people, culture, and work flow, we needed to adapt our traditional work format and environment. It needed to reflect our values, culture, and function.

Glass barriers

We had taken an intuitive approach to the original fit-out of the Back In Motion national office. There wasn't much strategic thought to how architecture or design might impact culture and work flow.

Most organisations put executives and managers in perimeter offices. Support staff sit in desk rows or cubicles in the centre. Meeting rooms and common areas are then scattered throughout.

We followed this traditional format. The Support Office looked like every other corporate office I had ever seen. It has been a cliché of workplaces over the decades that office size, location, and luxury, reflect authority, importance, and value. We thought so too.

When I was the 'boss', I had a reserved undercover carpark close to reception. I enjoyed the largest office. It was in the corner of the building. My executive assistant was the gatekeeper, sitting right outside. Inside my office I had a desk bigger than I needed. I had a lounge suite to host guests. A flat screen TV hung from the wall. I had a small board table to chair short meetings.

I was self-contained. People came to me. It was my sanctuary.

Except for toilet breaks, I could remain in my office all day: distant, unreachable, out of sight. Even though this was not my mindset, it was my environment. The format allowed it to be so.

This was true also of our executive and senior staff. Each had their own private office – with glass walls that created barriers to the team around them. You could look inside, but not walk through.

Elitism slowly crept into our culture.

Promotions were expected to be accompanied by an office. Moving from the open plan bullpen to a cubicle was evidence of a higher status. None of this happened with intent. This just happened to be the world we grew up in.

We ended up not liking it.

Space invaders

When our minds opened to a new way of thinking, our work spaces were immediately challenged.

Our leadership revolution had delivered new freedoms. We were all Colleagues now. There was no hierarchy, no elitism – no preference for one over another.

Support staff raised curious questions about seating arrangements. Carpark allocations got queried. Security access to different meeting rooms were reconsidered.

Our physical environment had to mirror our hearts. Our office layout had to encourage the very culture we were aspiring to.

After some animated conversations, we made some dramatic decisions:

- ► no private offices

- ► no reserved carparks

- ► no exclusive meeting rooms

- ► no restricted access.

Plaster and glass were demolished. Floor space was opened up. Everyone moved into an open environment. Colleagues were clustered in Functions. The desk layout echoed the lines of support and communication in our organisational chart.

Carparks became available on a first-come basis. More break-out spaces were created. Extra meeting rooms appeared.

We all had to change… some more than others. I lost my sanctuary in exchange for the bullpen. But I gained something greater – visibility, accessibility, alignment, congruence… relevance.

Death by meeting

With the physical surrounds adjusted, we were next forced to consider our meeting format.

Meetings are the black hole of organisational productivity. People take *minutes* in meetings, but often lose *hours*. Patrick Lencioni calls it *death by meeting*. We were stage 4 terminal. Our meetings were long… frequent… circular. They were fuelled by negative tension and animosity. They had become platforms of ego and opportunism.

We were wasting one of our most precious resources: time.

The unredeemable

As mentioned in Chapter 6, time, people, and money are our greatest tools for change. Of these three, I shamelessly listed time as the most important.

Money can be lost and made. People can be hurt and recover. But time is unredeemable. You can never recover the minutes, hours and days wasted. Once passed, time never returns.

And while time is the greatest resource at our disposal, people are the purpose we should live for. Time allows us to invest in people and make a difference.

Through finite time, we can be infinitely significant. Yet we were being frivolous with ours. So we reflected on what came to be known as the *time sphere*.

Time sphere

Every working day is made up of four primary demands (see Figure 8.1):

- *Boss*-imposed time: activities directed by superiors.
- *Team*-imposed time: activities negotiated and agreed among peers.
- *System*-imposed time: activities implied by your role.
- *Self*-imposed time: activities chosen at your own discretion.

In our original top-down management, we were distorted.

People's time was filled with external demands. The boss and the system prevailed. Few people had freedom to consider their best use of time. Others mostly drove activity. No space was provided for fresh contribution. There was no oxygen for initiative and creativity. People had little control and influence.

In hindsight, we had robbed ourselves. The best ideas come from open space, clear thought, and availability.

Figure 8.1: Time sphere *before* ONEteam™

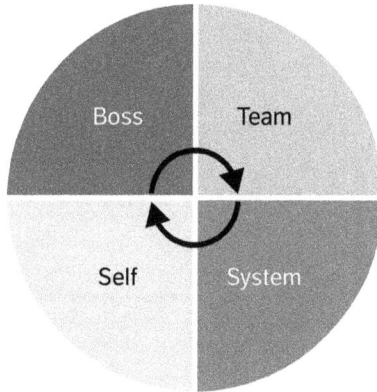

We needed to reshape the time sphere.

We wanted almost no boss-imposed activity. People should own their role. Serve the mission, not the man.

We wanted less system-imposed routine. Many people found themselves doing tasks for no sound reason, and only because they had always been done that way. There was no rationale, no understanding, and no benefit. It was like the system had taken over.

But we wanted more of the other two quadrants. We needed to promote more team- and self-imposed activities (see Figure 8.2 overleaf).

People can distinguish themselves and bring their best when given freedom to choose what they invest in.

To find more time, we had to steal it from somewhere. There was an obvious source. Ineffective meetings that consumed our daily schedule fell in the crosshairs.

Figure 8.2: Time sphere *after* ONEteam™

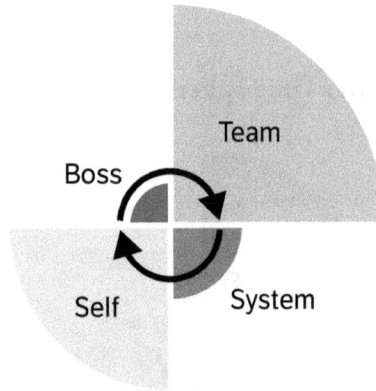

Our new rhythm

We introduced a radical new meeting format.

We agreed that everybody needed to get together formally only once a month. We called this our ONEteam™ meeting. This gathering was centred on relationship, alignment, and learning. The format would vary, but included professional development; strategic consultation; tactical planning; skills training; awards and acknowledgement; team building; and trend reporting.

Everybody was expected. No invitation was necessary.

As for all other meetings, the mantra was opposite. Everybody was invited, but no one was expected. Turn up if the meeting is relevant to you. Otherwise, don't. Decline if you can contribute to the team in better ways than spending time in the meeting.

We became accustomed to meeting at desks, standing up in the corridors, and making decisions in a gaggle of people gathered at the photocopier. Many opted to even walk the block with two or three others to discuss an idea or resolve a conflict.

We didn't close meeting room doors. We didn't speak in hushed tones afraid of who might overhear. There was no secret business.

Minutes were published in public document repositories. Flat screen TVs were installed to flash action plans and meeting outcomes. People didn't have to attend meetings to stay informed.

Our workspace relaxed, and so did our meeting rhythm. We changed our format – *outside-in downside-up*. Productivity improved. Time was recovered.

Close the loop

Not long into our ONEteam™ experience, we realised the best of intentions are not watertight. Some crucial information and details were slipping through the cracks because meetings were left to chance.

We needed to close the loop. So the LOOP meeting was born – silicon to gap seal our leaks.

Function Ambassadors gathered for a two-hour tactical work flow meeting each fortnight. Work Plans were shared. Respectful debate followed. Tensions were addressed. Collaborative decisions got made. Resources were allocated.

The facilitation responsibilities of each meeting were rotated. We had a different Chairperson every fortnight. Ultimately, peer accountability was encouraged. People connected. Wheels got aligned. We landed on one page.

We now had only two formal meetings each month to attend. Not 12, but two!

Daryl's story

A key difference between a typical organisational structure and our business is the way we host our meetings. It was a huge adjustment joining a new team and learning that the leaders you meet with are not necessarily *above* or *below* you, but would be contributing at the same level, on the same agenda items, as everybody else.

Like all meetings, they are not always fun. There are ups and downs, and moments when you wonder whether your time is effective. Having said this though, I have found the LOOP meetings to be framed with the best of intentions. They truly seek to create space for everyone to contribute. When we encourage discussion, debate, and analysis from a range of views we see the best versions of ourselves emerge.

This is a format that's continually changing. We keep adjusting our approach to ensure we land in that sweet spot between routine disclosure and meaningful discussion. My best experience is when I can walk out of the LOOP meeting and admit three things: (1) I learned something new; (2) I was able to contribute to the broader business; and (3) I felt we grew in unity as a team because we learned where each other was at.

I realise the LOOPs only work when I'm willing to invest myself into them.

Champions and Advocates

All other meetings are driven by need – not routine. There's no imposition, no formality.

Function Colleagues meet as needed to sharpen their focus and load-balance their Work Plan.

Advocates meet with Champions to challenge their thinking and hold them accountable.

Cross-Function peers form mini-LOOPs to round out smaller projects and interrelated tasks.

Anyone can call a meeting. Nobody needs special permission to attend. The need is defined by our organisational purpose and mission, not the calendar.

We were back in control.

Seatings and meetings

People might doubt the significance of these format changes. We are tempted to think seatings and meetings are benign elements of the workplace. This may be the case for some. But I doubt it. They mattered to our people. Format infers values and belief.

We had to avoid lip service. We had to spend money on these tangible changes to underscore importance. Change your environment and you effect change in perspective. Move your format and you can move mindsets. Shift seats and you will shift paradigms.

I no longer sat in a corner office. There was no hierarchy of workstations. Executive thrones had been overturned.

Exclusive meetings ended. Open dialogue was encouraged in real time. Everyone was invited into the inner circle.

We became nimble, agile, flexible, goal-orientated. Old ways had all but lost their grip. Outcomes and actions were now paramount. Our format was aligned with our purpose.

The change was nearly complete. Almost!

Transferable Principles

42 Format and environment should promote *values, culture,* and *function.*

43 Time is *unredeemable.* It should be jealously guarded and purposefully invested.

44 People *take minutes* in meetings, but often *lose hours.* Only attend meetings that are relevant to you.

45 Avoid *boss-* and *system*-imposed activities in favour of *team-* and *self*-imposed priorities.

9. CHANGE

Soul equity

Everything worthwhile requires investment. Nothing ventured, nothing gained. The universal law of proportionate risk and return governs our world.

If you want to change your destiny, you need to change your behaviour. The inescapable truth is that progress relies on change. This is true for Back In Motion, as with the rest of the world. We accepted that if we did not change our direction, our team trajectory would take us somewhere we didn't want to go.

We had to be courageous – risk the safe, and launch into the unknown. Our ONEteam™ revolution demanded change in ways we initially thought impossible. It was hard work. We spilt blood, sweat, and tears.

We invested more of ourselves into this adventure than anything else before. It mattered – supremely. It cost us time, money, ego, position, comfort. But it won us freedom.

We recovered *team. Leverage* became our friend again. *Collaboration* flowed. *Results* were achieved. You can't buy these outcomes. And if you could, nobody could afford them.

We bought our prize through sweat equity. And we invested a lot of soul equity, too.

Bullfrogs and butterflies

Long-lasting effective change is painful. We all know this in theory. Nature calls it metamorphosis: the process of transformation from immaturity to an adult form.

We were like tadpoles en route to becoming proud bullfrogs. Or caterpillars morphing, step by step, through pupal stages, until we were ready to fly. We had to grow up – fast – as a team, and as individuals.

Frankly, a lot of the time we felt lost in the dark... in our very own cocoons. Nobody could speed this up or slow it down for us. It was our change to live through. It had to happen from deep within. Our change in behaviour began with a change in the heart.

Eventually, light gave way. We saw where we were heading. The payoff was ahead.

Brain change

Research shows that 72% of all attempted change fails. The statistics are discouraging. The prognosis is poor.

We fail for many reasons. There are many 'un's... unmotivated, undisciplined, unplanned, unaccountable, unsupported, unexpectant.

All things are created thrice. Firstly, in the *heart*; then in the *mind*; and, eventually, in *reality*. Mostly we fail in the brain before we fail in action. Neuroleadership, psychology, and behavioural science have much to teach us in explaining human behaviour and the effects of change.

Our workforce became students of these matters. We learned not to fear change, but to embrace it. Change became our constant.

The great realisation was that change at work is inevitable; but progress is optional. That is, not all change is positive and constructive.

It was on us to make it purposeful, rather than change becoming benign (or worse!).

We had a choice. We could take some chances and lead this revolution on our terms. Or we could let fate run its course and deal with the consequences. Either way, change was coming.

We decided to change the changeable; accept the unchangeable; and resist the unacceptable.

You can too.

Jake's story

When I first joined Back In Motion, the ONEteam™ model had been in play for only a few months. I remember thinking it was the epitome of three-letter acronyms and some clever slogans to create a perception more than a reality.

It took about six months for me to find my rhythm in this unique model. I quickly realised there was more to this business approach than I originally suspected. I was invited to speak on strategic plans and decision-making despite being a lower level talent. I was able to comment on our budget and financial plans. I had full access to all aspects of business information (profitability, expenses, etc.), and I was able to contribute my areas of strength in a welcoming environment.

It seemed like business intelligence was up, and individuals developed their experience at rates far more rapid than in traditional workplace structures. Some decisions took longer to make, but the outcome was better than if it had received fewer touch points.

In the end, I have been able to develop my career by stepping from one Function to another with relative ease. Jason calls it 'choose your own adventure'. Because of our collaborative, open-plan work style, I was able to develop insights into other Functions of the business that eventually presented as a new career opportunity to me. This would have been much harder in a traditional hierarchy, as you tend to get pigeon-holed and profiled quickly in a certain line of expertise.

Although I think the learning curve of ONEteam™ was steep, the team and I are better for the experience. Most importantly though, I believe our franchisees and workforce have benefited the most, given that we as the national team are empowered to bring our best contribution every day for their benefit.

Red wine

Our quirky story of leadership revolution simply narrates a journey of growth. Our slow crawl toward commercial adulthood. Inescapable lessons we had to learn to become better.

Our success was determined by how many uncomfortable conversations and circumstances we were willing to confront every day.

Wisdom came with experience, and we were having lots of new experiences. Like a good wine, we were maturing with age. We learned to believe in ourselves, and not be dictated to by our circumstances. We measurably increased our capacity and tolerance for strain and discomfort. And we saw change as a growth opportunity.

But that same bottle of vintage red could still cork if we weren't careful. We had to continuously guard against being careless with matters of the heart; resisting new things; and complaining, criticising, or blaming others.

Iceberg paradigm

Ultimately, this entire experience relied on *leadership*. The clichéd, overused, and poorly understood attribute that apparently all workplaces depend on… even strive for.

Leadership!

This wasn't a management restructure, cultural programme, or engagement strategy. As we say, it was a leadership revolution. But not just plain-wrap, vanilla leadership. It was the stuff of icebergs.

Grade four science class taught me that only one tenth of an iceberg appears above the surface – the colloquial 'tip'. Pop culture tempts us to believe that superficial attributes define us – the visible skills, qualifications, and personality traits. That the way we dress, talk, and walk – the image we project – is representative of the whole.

But the tip of our iceberg doesn't define us. It deceives us. The real *you* lives under the surface. Just as the real mass of an iceberg is submerged, so lies 90% of the attributes of an effective leader. They are deep on the inside – well beneath the water level.

Leadership that emerges from the substance and architecture of our inner world is more compelling and influential than any credential, corner office, workplace title, or inflated remuneration package. Leadership based on the iceberg paradigm drives change from the heart and soul. Deep within.

The team at Back In Motion recognised this. We developed the lost art of visioneering – setting direction with clarity and purpose. We laboured the efforts of gaining commitment from the kindred spirits within the team, never leaving a (wo)man down on the battlefield.

We relentlessly pursued our goal for change – *over*-leading, and *under*-managing.

We expected everyone to lead when they were naturally the right person to do so – with no exceptions. Why? Because everything rises and falls on virtuous leadership.

Spin cycle

Embedded within the experience shared in this book is a lifetime of learning compacted into two intense years.

It was something of a paradox. Our journey was emotionally charged, yet very pragmatic. It resolved tensions, while at the same time was provocative and confrontational. We were drawn together in new and unique ways, even though the beliefs themselves threatened to separate us at times.

This was not a straightforward journey of change. It was not incremental, linear, or predictable in any way. It was like tumbling haphazardly in a workplace washing-machine. All of the colours were mixed. Delicates were included with the heavily stained and soiled garments. The spin cycle was enduring.

We were turned *outside-in* and *downside-up*. But fortunately, we washed well.

Remember, not everyone has to experience our same pain – or the extremes of our change. You can learn from our story. You are not all in the same situation we found ourselves. And if you are, your team composition and aspiration are undoubtedly different.

For this reason, the specific model of ONEteam", as I describe in this book, is unlikely to be a perfect fit for you. I'm not prescribing this workplace model as the only, or even the best, suggestion for you to implement. It's not designed as a 'plug and play' accessory to your current organisational structure, like many of us wish it were.

ONEteam" is simply our story of transformation. And what became important to us along the way.

Outside-in downside-up leadership

Whatever you decide, it's crucial you don't miss the underlying attributes of *outside-in downside-up* leadership that enabled our success. It wasn't our planetary model *per se*, that benefited us so profoundly. Pods, Champions, Functions, Role Profiles, and Full Circle Development Plans are merely assets we developed to serve our greater mission. Structure is inert in itself... just a device in the hands of its masters to best reflect cultural identity and intent.

Our true discovery was not the ONEteam" model, but rather the heart and disposition of any great team – the true soul of an effective workplace.

Figure 9.1 summarises the 10 organisational truths we committed ourselves to. It's our distilled wisdom from everything we learned on this great adventure of ONEteam™. These underlying attributes are what energise every high-performing, self-governing, and values-driven team. They empower people to love what they do, and love who they do it with.

Figure 9.1: The fundamental attributes of
outside-in downside-up **leadership which underlie**
the ONEteam™ model

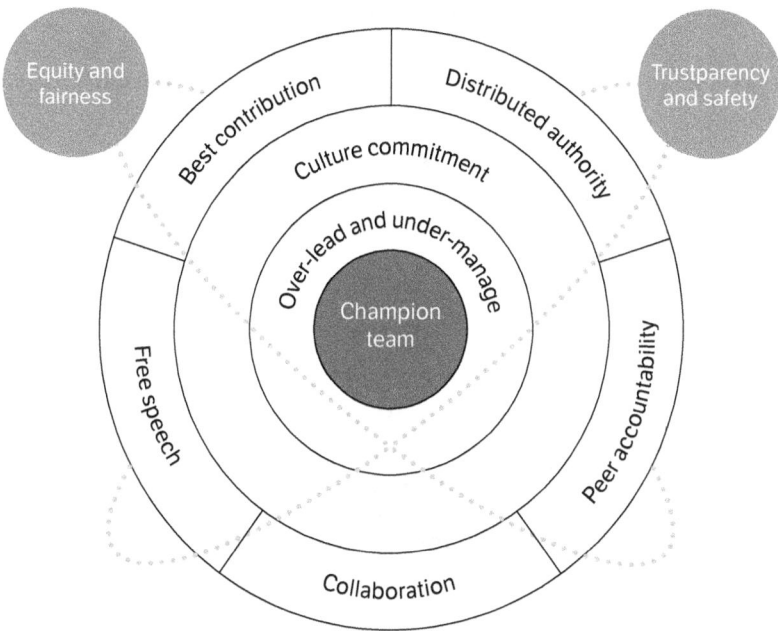

The 10 attributes that best represent authentic *outside-in downside-up* leadership are:

1. **Create a champion team (not a team of champions)** – Individual excellence does not equate to superior team performance. Superstars and rainmakers should not be elevated above the importance of the collective. A true team is a remarkable phenomenon worth fighting for, and comes when individuals place the best interests of the team above themselves.

2. **Over-lead and under-manage** – Each one should lead when they are naturally the right person to do so. In my experience, no one has ever been criticised for leading too much, but often we are warned about the perils of micro-managing others. The sentiment is simple. Lead more, and manage less. The latter is relied upon as a proxy for the former, and is a very poor substitute.

3. **Culture Commitment** – Every team must agree on how it is going to behave. Intentionally outline the *modus operandi* so the ground rules are clear. Commit to doing what you said you were going to do, and take ownership as though it all came down to you. Set expectations early, do not tolerate serial violations, and celebrate the right choices.

4. **Distributed authority** – Empower those in the right position, with the right skills, to make the right decisions. Push the authority as close to the front line of the organisation as possible, while ensuring optimal outcomes.

5. **Peer accountability** – This is the holy grail of team culture. Every person has to be willing to give and receive instruction, correction, and encouragement in ways that make upper levels of management and oversight increasingly redundant. The best of me should bring out the best in you, irrespective of our positions.

6. **Collaboration** – The policy should be clear: no secrets; no surprises; no politics; no hype; no selfish posturing; and no

empty promises. Everybody on the team must work together for the common good. Don't separate, isolate, fragment, or silo the valuable knowledge, skills, and efforts. Doing so will only dilute and diminish the team's effectiveness. Choose to listen, communicate, and learn without prejudice and with an open mind.

7. **Free speech** – If you *think* it, it's inevitable at some point you will *act* it. So it's better to *speak* it. Every opinion should be considered in collective review. Respectful debate should be encouraged. Everyone needs to have an opportunity to voice their views. Speak up at the right time, with the right people, in the right way.

8. **Best contribution** – Team members should not be limited by titles and static job descriptions, but enabled to serve the team with their fluid skills and abilities as they might be called or relied upon. Play each one to their strengths for the benefit of the team.

9. **Trustparency and safety** – Every person should act in a trustworthy manner, on a want-to-know basis, and make others feel safe in the way they lead and seek to have influence.

10. **Equity and fairness** – Teams are rarely made up of identical people. We all contribute different skills and experiences. We each make unique contributions. Accordingly, each will benefit from different rewards and opportunities. But while we are not equal, there should be equity. Even though we are not all the same, we should seek and promote fairness. We should consider others as we and they would like to be treated.

If you can apply these attributes in whatever workplace model you prefer, the experience will be rich and fulfilling. Violate these attributes, and the consequences will be real and disabling.

In our experience, the ONEteam™ model provided a means for us to promote these 10 attributes in a way that became natural – even habitual.

The value wasn't found in the structure; the structure was founded on these values.

Mirror image

So what do you value? How does your world need to change? What revolution needs to be started in your workplace? How are you going to lead?

Look in the mirror rather than through the glass. What do you see?

Examine your heart and test your mind. Reconcile the ideal with the possible. Give permission to your imagination to dream big.

Whatever you do, learn how to anticipate change. Adapt quickly, and enjoy the struggle.

And remember, whatever you see in the mirror will reproduce after its own kind. You will get more of the same. The farmers of old teach us the rule of harvest. We reap what we sow. So, either love what you see and embrace more of it… or commit to change at the innermost level first.

Start with self. Others will follow. The tipping point will inevitably come.

Live on purpose. Change with intent.

Vive la liberté

Love, protection, food, shelter: Abraham Maslow counted them among the basic human needs in his psychology classic. But right up there is also our longing for freedom… including freedom within the workplace. Maybe, in our modern world of corporate institutionalisation, this is more so the case in the workplace than anywhere else.

Back In Motion bred a new race of freedom fighters. You could too.

On the inside we wore camouflage, black paint under the eyes, and artillery belts. We slept draped in the flag of our cause. We were highly educated, respected, white collar guerrillas. We fought against our own traditions, our flawed habits, and our ineffective strategies of the past.

The call was clear; burn the bridges. Scuttle the boats. With no retreat – conquer or die.

Back In Motion gained its independence in 2013. Because of ONEteam™, we will never be the same.

It was hard fought, but we won the battle. Even if the war drags on!

Vive la liberté. Long live freedom. Don't fear *outside-in downside-up* leadership. Embrace the cause.

Go now, and incite your very own leadership revolution!

Transferable Principles

46. Change is *inevitable*, progress is *optional.* Make it purposeful rather than benign (or worse!).

47. All things are created thrice. Firstly, in the *heart*; then the *mind*; and, eventually, in *reality.*

48. Our superficial workplace attributes don't *define* us. They *deceive* us. The heart and soul of our team lies deep within.

49. If you want to change your *destiny,* you need to change your *behaviour.*

50. Create a *champion team* over a *team of champions.*

FINAL WORD

Leading teams is a dangerous occupation. Sun Tzu called it the *art of war*. The fight for hearts and minds. It's about standing up and being heard in a noisy world. The marketplace is full of competing opinions, experiences, and ideals. Skilfully navigating a team through it all is a masterful craft that evades most.

And it is clear too, I still have much to learn.

At the time of writing, the Back In Motion Health Group can boast some wonderful achievements. It is an award-winning international franchise network in the coveted allied health sector. It has a mature domestic footprint in most states of Australia. It has launched in New Zealand. There are burgeoning opportunities in North America and the UK. We have launched speciality sub-brands. We have a professional workforce of over 600 people. We deliver over half a million services to valued clientele every year. And we are about to apply our model in new health markets as we integrate and synthesise our learnings.

As for our Strategic Target of 7/50/100, we achieved brand presence in 7 states or territories, generated revenues close to $50 million in annual client services, and now officially host over 110 locations. Given only about half of our locations are full-service flagship practices, we continue to pursue this element of our original target.

The Colleagues leading our organisation still work together as one team – that is, ONEteam¨.

ONEteam™ looks different now to how it started. In another year or two, it will change again.

We must keep practising, to get it right. Like learning to drive a car – it first starts with doing it very intentionally and cerebrally, and slowly, over time, it becomes automatic. But we must keep re-engineering the vehicle for high performance.

What worked *then*, will probably not work *now*. New strategies will get us from *here* to *there*.

And for those who wonder if it gets easier over time, it does! But we don't continue with ONEteam™ because it's easy.

As the owner, I would find it much easier to resume an old model of traditional hierarchy. I could comfortably slip into the posture of benevolent autocracy again. It would be no effort to become the centre of attention, controlling all of the initiatives, making all of the decisions, reclaiming a large corner office, and enjoying a reserved carpark at the front door. I can be tempted with the allure of control most other days.

Life in the business would be unambiguous, more process-driven, predictable, easier, and faster. But it most certainly would not be better!

ONEteam™ was never designed as the *easy* option… or, as the *final* option. It was just promoted as the most *superior* one to date!

But we all must continue to learn and innovate.

One of the greatest challenges we still wrestle with in the ONEteam™ model is how to facilitate individuals through a self-directed path of career progression. We want them to advance in knowledge, experience, responsibility, and earning. But we don't have a linear, top-down structure that presents an obvious pathway for this. We don't want one!

What we want is the more creative, intuitive, and tailored opportunities embedded within a non-linear path. Growing in tangential ways that serve the mission should be rewarded more than just climbing a basic ladder. The former relies on flexibility and more disruptive thinking.

We haven't solved this challenge fully. It remains an elusive part of our great adventure. It is just one example of us not having all of the answers – but also not stopping the search. We are on a limitless journey in pursuit of authentic workplace leadership and self-actualisation. So, the hunt continues! *Outside-in* and *downside-up*.

This book describes only our experience to date. We will keep living, working, and evolving ONEteam™ as a leadership model. It will change, as we do. We need it to!

(As I wonder, you might too…?)

List of Transferable Principles

1. A clear *identity* will fuel personal *motivation* and *purpose*.

2. Your identity must be *clear, memorable,* and *transferable* to those around you.

3. Beware of *vision leaks* and *mission drift.* Organisational *size* becomes the enemy of collective *direction* and *alignment.*

4. A change in *circumstances* often gives you a change in *perspective.*

5. Organisational *structure* must reflect and serve organisational *identity.*

6. The best form of leadership is *truth.*

7. Without *progressive change*, you may become a victim of your own success.

8. Teams thrive on *over*-leadership and *under*-management.

9. *Invite* people into change, rather than *demand* it from them.

10. Collaboration is *multiplication.*

11. Don't confuse *ownership* with *leadership.*

12. As operational visibility and responsibilities *decrease,* leadership presence must *increase.*

13. Beware workplace titles – as they can often be *ambiguous, incomplete,* and *self-limiting.* Encourage *best contribution* instead.

14. Prefer platforms of *influence* over positions of *authority.*

15. If people *think* it, they will eventually *act* it. So, encourage free speech early and respectfully.

16. Don't confuse *equity* with equality. Value *fairness* over sameness.

17. Organisational structure is not *good* or *bad* – it's just executed *rightly* or *wrongly*.

18. Change can be led by *evolution* or *revolution* – choose carefully.

19. Every organisation has an *axis* of *identity* – just not necessarily the one they chose.

20. The manager must *decrease*, so the team can *increase*.

21. Serve an organisational *mission*; not a literal man or woman.

22. Distributed authority empowers *freedom* and *responsibility*.

23. Culture eats *strategy* for breakfast, *vision* for lunch, and *structure* for dinner.

24. *Teams* create culture, not just leaders.

25. Trust is earned when *actions* meet *words*.

26. Most leaders *assume* their culture is *better* than it really is.

27. If you are not intentionally building a *specific* culture, then you are unintentionally building an *alternative* one.

28. To change culture, people need *actionable* first steps.

29. Culture must become a *commitment*. It's not *set-and-forget*. It's a decision that must be refreshed daily.

30. The mechanics of work flow matter. At some point the *thinking* must convert to *doing*.

31. *Less* is best. The fewer priorities, the more likely you will *retain focus* and *achieve* them.

32. Workplace leadership is a *team sport*, so it needs a *scoreboard* – lead and lag measures.

33. Vision must be resourced – so plan and budget for *people, time,* and *money*!

34. Embrace *trust*parency. Nurture a *want-to-know* culture rather than keeping people on a *need-to-know* basis.

35. It's all about the people. They are the collective soul of the workplace. They are both the *means* and the *end* to achieving vision.

36. *Being* well precedes *doing* well.

37. Replace lines of *report* with lines of *support*.

38. Immediate consensus is not the sign of a great team. *Respectful candour* and *rigorous debate* reflects true team maturity.

39. At the heart of the social team contract is *fair reward*.

40. Every fair workplace system must provide a *right of appeal*.

41. *Peer accountability* is the holy grail of team leadership. The *best of me* should elicit the *best of you*.

42. Format and environment should promote *values, culture,* and *function*.

43. Time is *unredeemable*. It should be jealously guarded and purposefully invested.

44. People *take minutes* in meetings, but often *lose hours*. Only attend meetings that are relevant to you.

45. Avoid *boss-* and *system*-imposed activities in favour of *team-* and *self*-imposed priorities.

46. Change is *inevitable*, progress is *optional*. Make it purposeful rather than benign (or worse!).

47. All things are created thrice. Firstly, in the *heart*; then the *mind*; and eventually, in *reality*.

48. Our superficial workplace attributes don't *define* us. They *deceive* us. The heart and soul of our team lies deep within.

49. If you want to change your *destiny*, you need to change your *behaviour*.

50. Create a *champion team* over a *team of champions*.

Glossary

Advisory Board means the non-executive governance forum within the Support Ring of ONEteam™.

Advocate means the coach of the Function.

Ambassador means the most appropriate Colleague to act on behalf of or as representative of a Function or Pod for a defined purpose.

Associate Lead means the supporting facilitator(s) of ONEteam™.

Board Chair means the chair of the Advisory Board.

Champion means the captain of the Function.

Colleague means a member of ONEteam™.

Core Work Description means the essential roles, responsibilities, and contributions ONEteam™ relies on the Colleague to perform.

Culture Commitment means the behaviours each Colleague has agreed to be held accountable to.

Executive Lead means the principal facilitator of ONEteam™.

First Level Support (1S) means the Colleague nominated in a Role Profile to provide initial formal support to another Colleague.

Full Circle Development Plan (FCDP) means an individual document to assist in the professional growth, career planning, and talent optimisation of a Colleague.

Function means a specific domain of technical expertise and specialised knowledge that provides important organisational capability to ONEteam™.

Governance Charter means the document outlining the structure, roles, responsibilities, policies, and processes of the ONEteam™ leadership philosophy, outlining the 'rules of the game'.

LOOP means a meeting of Function, Pod, and Support Ring Ambassadors to report on and discuss key matters of business operation, 'closing the loop'.

Mandate means the key objective of each Function, Pod, Support Ring, or Advisory Board that the rest of ONEteam™ relies on to deliver in order to collectively achieve MPV_1SV_2.

MPV_1SV_2 means the identity acronym for Mission, Purpose, Vision, Strategy, Values.

ONEteam™ means the organisational system created for governance of, and leadership within, the Back In Motion organisation.

ONEteam™ Policies are specific standards, expectations, processes, or systems published to assist and guide Colleagues in the fulfilment of the Governance Charter.

Owner(s) means the shareholder(s) of the organisation.

Pod means a permanent leadership group working on behalf of and orbiting ONEteam™, commissioned by the LOOP with a specific Mandate.

Pod Chairperson means the principal facilitator of the Pod.

Project means the special-purpose activities of Colleagues within the ONEteam™ structure to deliver on specified objectives in a finite timeframe.

Project Lead means the Colleague who takes ultimate responsibility for a Project.

Role Profile means the document outlining a Colleague's agreed contribution to ONEteam™.

Round Table means a live 360 degree performance appraisal as part of a Colleague's Full Circle Development Plan.

Second Level Support (2S) means the Colleague nominated in a Role Profile to provide secondary formal support to another Colleague.

Secondary Work Description means the adjunctive and supportive roles, responsibilities, and contributions ONEteam™ relies upon the Colleague to perform.

Support Ring means those Colleagues whose Core Work Description is to unite and optimise the Functions and Pods to achieve MPV_1SV_2.

Taskforce means a temporary special-purpose forum typically inclusive of stakeholders outside of the ONEteam™ structure to deliver on specified objectives in a finite timeframe.

Third Level Support (3S) means the Colleagues of the Support Ring as the third back up to provide formal support to other Colleagues.

Work Plan means an active record of prioritised projects, recurring tasks, measurable outcomes, and deferred initiatives to strategically serve MPV_1SV_2.

Suggested Reading

Here are some other titles that exemplify the courage of creative and unconventional workplace models.

Hsieh, T. (2010) *Delivering Happiness: A Path to Profits, Passion and Purpose.* Grand Central Publishing.

Hughes, B. and Klein, S. (2015) *Blinkracy: A Step-by-Step Guide to Make Any Company Management-Free and 100% Results-Oriented.*

Kirkpatrick, D. (2011) *Beyond Empowerment: The Age of the Self-Managed Organization.* Morning Star Self-Management Institute.

Laloux, F. (2014) *Reinventing Organisations: A Guide to Creating Organizations Inspired by the Next Stage in Human Consciousness.* Nelson Parker.

Marquet, L.D. (2013) *Turn the Ship Around! A True Story of Turning Followers Into Leaders.* Portfolio.

McChrystal, S. (2015) *Team of Teams: New Rules of Engagement for a Complex World.* Portfolio Hardcover.

Robertson, B.J. (2015) *Holacracy: The New Management System for a Rapidly Changing World.* Henry Holt and Co.

Semler, R. Maverick (2001) *The Success Story Behind the World's Most Unusual Workplace.* Random House.

Whitehurst, J. (2015) *The Open Organization: Igniting Passion and Performance.* Harvard Business Review Press.

Index

About the Author

Jason T. Smith
www.jasonterencesmith.com

Jason is a driving force: a dynamic business and health thought leader, award-winning entrepreneur, and acclaimed physiotherapist.

He founded the **Back In Motion Health Group** (www.backin motion.com.au) from his garage in 1999. Jason now leads a team of more than 600 professionals in over 100 locations across Australia and New Zealand. He has made a career out of radically challenging the norm and pioneering fresh business paradigms. The results speak volumes. Jason was the Ernst & Young Entrepreneur of the Year 2013 for Services in the Southern region. And Back In Motion has become Australia's largest and fastest growing provider of physiotherapy and related services – awarded the BRW Fast Franchise for five consecutive years.

Jason shares his vision, drive, and expertise through **active leadership** in peak bodies, community organisations, CEO groups, and special interest business forums in Australia and beyond. He sits on multiple corporate and NFP boards, and consults widely on leadership, strategy, and governance.

Passionate about the power of effective leadership, Jason established the **Iceberg Leadership Institute**. Thousands of aspiring and experienced professionals have benefited from his thought-provoking mentorship since its inception (www.icebergleadership.com.au).

Jason's first book, *Get Yourself Back In Motion: a physiotherapist's secrets to pain relief and optimal health*, was an international best-seller. He regularly appears in the media as a popular contributor and presenter on health, wellness, and business-related subjects. As a charismatic and inspiring **keynote speaker**, Jason has presented to over 50,000 people internationally.

Jason is unrelentingly committed to improving outcomes for those less fortunate. He works with many welfare organisations and community groups, most notably as the Chair of the **SOS Health Foundation** which serves to improve the health of disadvantaged Australians (www.soshealth.org.au).

A proud **father** to four young children, Jason loves spending time with his family. He also enjoys playing tennis, riding his Harley Davidson motorbike, travelling, and adventure seeking, and is active in his local Christian Church community.

Other Titles

Available in paperback, eBook, and audio at jasontsmith.com.au

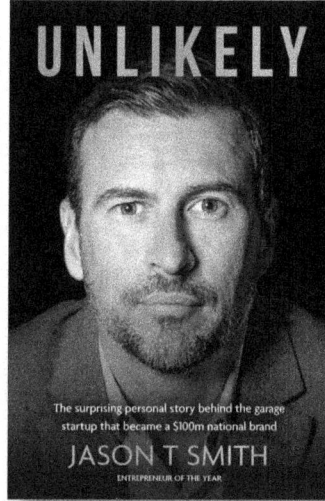

Follow Jason on social media

www.ingramcontent.com/pod-product-compliance
Lightning Source LLC
Chambersburg PA
CBHW032329210326
41518CB00041B/1987